No Parent Is An Island
second edition
by
Paula Johanson

While every precaution has been taken in the preparation of this book, the publisher assumes no responsibility for errors or omissions, or for damages resulting from the use of the information contained herein.

NO PARENT IS AN ISLAND

First edition. March 31, 2023.

Copyright © 2023 Paula Johanson.

ISBN: 978-1989966266

Written by Paula Johanson.

For all my family

For all my dear friends

Splendid Isolation

There isn't much about having a family that's unique. We're born into families; most of us are raised in families and go on to start or choose our own. But when I began my own family, it did seem unique. All these exciting and dull and frustrating and peaceful things were happening around me. And when I wanted to talk about all of it, there was usually no one around to talk with – no one, that is, who wouldn't answer with insightful comments like "Gollygollygolly" or "People have toes." So I started writing.

When our twins were born – yes, twins, we do nothing by halves in this family – we were living in Victoria, BC in a downtown industrial neighbourhood, in a duplex which formerly had been a fine old 1910 house. Although the neighbours on either side were six feet away and could look into our living room and kitchen windows if they so chose, it was astonishingly quiet and peaceful to live there.

There were a dozen old houses on both sides of the block, surrounded by light industry. The brick yard and warehouses at the end of the next block were not noisy; the gas station and glass cutter were even quieter, and every few weeks a worker from the Soap Products warehouse would come out and hose down the suds that piled up in their receiving bay on a rainy day.

We could walk in that neighbourhood for a mile in a spiral of streets, never seeing a single human being, while traffic on two major roads roared by, two blocks away. When we told people where we lived, their usual response was: "But there isn't anything between Bay Street and Gorge Road! Doesn't the harbour come right up there?" Sometimes living there felt like splendid isolation. Sometimes it felt like living in forgotten territory. Those feelings had a lot to do with raising children where no one expected to see them – next door to a rhythm & blues band, strolleringly downtown to the provincial museum, or walking around the corner to the cathedral full of old people.

The rent was low, there was a small yard for the toddlers, and a basement for my husband, Bernie's, woodworking. I wrote three novels, two dozen stories and a stack of poems; two of the stories and some poems sold to magazines. We stayed for five years while other families gradually moved away, and the tone of the little neighbourhood began to change. When we moved away, we didn't end up in the suburbs with a Yuppie lifestyle. Bernie and I hardly qualify for Yuppies or a mortgage. We moved to his parents' farm, almost fifty miles north of Edmonton, Alberta.

You want to talk splendid isolation? The nearest neighbour was half a mile away. Our mailbox was a full mile away. The dozen houses of our entire former neighbourhood could have fit on our new lawn of rough grass around the tiny farmhouse now filled with two five-year-olds, a woodworker and a writer.

You want to talk forgotten territory? Most of the old farmhouses for miles around were empty. The owners would come out in spring, plow their quarter or half sections of land (a section of land is a square, one mile on each side), plant grain, spray for weeds in summer, and harvest the grain in early fall. People who had "moved to town" or had always lived there talked of our family living on the farm in winter as if we were heroic, or foolish.

At times it was heroic. Just shovelling the driveway was a task for Hercules. Bernie used a tractor after snowfalls, and I would clear wind drifts with a manure shovel. The kids loved the heaps of snow and used them for sliding and building snow forts.

And yes, at times it was foolish. With temperatures of -40°C every winter, the children had to be taught new safety rules. Number one: "Don't Lick Metal!" (All Prairie kids try this once.) Number two: "Tell us before you go out to play in the field!" (One hundred and sixty acres, some of it bush, is enough to get lost in.) The one that didn't make sense to them at first was, "If no one else is home, stay indoors!"

Think about it. Two six-year-olds coming home on the schoolbus, arrive to an empty house because Mom and Dad drove to town to get groceries and got caught in a snowstorm. If the kids sit down to eat peanut butter sandwiches and watch cartoons, no problem. Even if the power and heat go out, they have blankets and food. The parents can concentrate on getting home safely.

We didn't have any disasters on the farm, and we lived there for four summers, learning market gardening and keeping our expenses low while

Bernie got his training in fine furniture making. I wrote two and a half novels, and began writing book reviews and articles. Many of the articles became this book.

Some of the experience of being a stay-at-home parent is similarly splendid isolation – a time away from work for pay, a time away from the rest of the world to focus on the child or children. Sometimes there is no relief from paid work and worldly concerns, yet child care must go on, even when no one else seems to understand the strange new focus of a parent's life – dynamic professionals suddenly hanging around parks and babbling while playing on the swings.

Some of the experience of being a parent is forgotten territory – just how many two am feedings is anyone willing to remember? Parents of grown children often leave that part of their lives behind when they move on to new concerns. And some people just never think about parents and children at all, as if they never had been affected! For example, it used to be a lot harder to get a stroller across roads and onto high curbs before traffic engineers began making accessible ramps for differently-abled people.

Some of that attitude of "Parenting as Forgotten Territory" is what I wrote about in these articles for *Island Parent*, *Transitions*, the *Bon Accord News*, *Single Minds*, and *Between Gynes*. But I have tried to write about the splendid isolation also – and how I felt when the crawling twins ate a jar of Vaseline, or the morning my three-year-old daughter, Lila, taught me to sing "Twelve Sticky Buns" while we played hooky from work and daycare, or the day we called 911.

What Did I Have?

No one will ever make a movie of the day I gave birth to twins. For one thing, a series of slides showing dream-like images would better represent my birthing experience. And people in a theatre would never feel that kick inside. But while we were pregnant, when my husband and I curled up together, we found that Bernie could get kicked just about as hard as me; and when I gave birth, Bernie was there, holding my right hand, keeping me focused, while outside the February weather rained, blew clear and sunny, and snowed and hailed by turns.

If the ultrasound scan hadn't told us to expect twins, I would have known it long before they were born. The morning one of them somersaulted while the other curled still was a clue. Another clue was playing "kick-tickle" with the four little feet we could trace through the stretched skin under my ribs.

The high-tech circus images began when I was strapped into two fetal monitors, with two screens beeping in the labour room. Bernie called the nurse once, saying, "This monitor shows zero for heart beat. Now, I know it's just because the baby moved, but tell us anyway!" We knew about monitors, because I'd gone into labour eight weeks early, on New Year's Eve. The labour had been stopped then. I went home with a bottle of pills and instructions not to give birth for at least three weeks.

Our friend Bev did so much to help then, cleaned house, scrubbed my bathtub sparkling, and prepared to join Bernie as my labour coach. I would drift off into daydreams from one moment to the next while Bernie and I were getting the nursery ready. The next thing I'd hear was "Hello! You were in Bermuda again." Well, it beat painting the walls. As I came around a corner another afternoon, Bernie commented to a friend, "Ah! She just hove into view!" Maybe my belly had swollen like the mainsail on a three-masted schooner but Linda didn't have to laugh that hard.

Never mind. Bernie and Bev encouraged me every day as I hung onto the babies for six more weeks. ("Oops," said the doctor, "I didn't really want to have you take those pills for four weeks, only two. Oh well, two weeks early is just right for twins.") I spent the last week resting in a hospital bed, puffy with retained water. Finally the doc broke my waters. Bev even remembered to remind my doctor and obstetrician that I wouldn't need a full dose of any pain killers, as half-doses are more than enough for me. Bernie and I told them also, more than once.

Even so, when the doctor gave me "just enough Demerol to make you relax and feel drowsy," it knocked me out for six hours. But not before mumbling, "I'm sorry there are so many socks all over my bedroom floor, Doctor." Hallucinations. One hallmark of an interesting birthing experience. My blood pressure soared.

The next I knew was a blur of voices and people, intruding on the birthing. I could see but not focus, and hear but not understand. Couldn't talk or sit up. Where were Bernie and Bev?

"Oh, we've got a good spread on her," the obstetrician was saying, patting my thighs. "But I'm worried all this edema will get in the way." Grrr. Who the hell was he talking to, instead of me? I turned my drug-fogged head to look around. Leaning up against the blurry white walls of the operating room was a whole row of medical students. They looked like a bunch of guys with a pack of cigarettes rolled up in the sleeves of their white t-shirts, one foot up on the bumper of a '61 Chevy with the hood up. "Yep," I expected to hear one of these yobs say, "looks like those valves will need re-lapping." Where were Bernie and Bev?

Scrubbing and gowning, as it turned out. The doctor didn't tell anyone that they were allowed in - finally half an hour later Bernie just followed a nurse in, and Bev came, too.

The nurses were trying to get me to push. The doctor and the obstetrician hadn't said a word to me. Not one. They were lucky I couldn't talk. I wanted to cuss them out. It felt like I was giving birth all by myself with intrusions of nightmare images from someone else's dreams: machines, straps and chemicals. I wasn't seeing or hearing clearly until Bernie took my hand and leaned over me. "All right, Beautiful!" he said. "Let's pop those puppies and blow this popsicle stand."

Bev took my left hand, careful of the IV needle. I couldn't see her, but I could smell her clean hair among all those hospital smells, and I latched on. Now I could let things happen. The obstetrician decided that an episiotomy and forceps were needed, and, in a slippery rush, my son was born.

A cry of delight went up from Bernie, Bev and the nurses. Bernie told Frank Bernhard Klassen his name. Ben turned his head to follow Bernie's voice with his blurry eyes.

Bev had told me that before she had her own kids, she had been looking forward to having a flat tummy again. She wasn't sure when it was supposed to happen – right after the birth or in a few hours. (Anyone looking at her own tummy is laughing now, right?) When I rested, unconscious, for half an hour, Bev noticed something she hadn't expected. The soft skin of my belly settled down around the remaining twin, showing the outline of the curled infant.

When my belly hardened into a dome again, I didn't wake up enough to push. Bernie had to wake me up, and speak right into my face. We were so angry with the doc and the OB: neither had said so much as one word to me. Was I okay? Was the second baby okay? They didn't say. The nurses glared at them, furious, Bev told me. The second birth was as blurry as the first. The medical students, all in a row, were still there. Bev reported to me later indignantly, "They looked like a bunch of guys with a pack of cigarettes rolled up in the sleeves of their white t-shirts, one foot up on the bumper of a '61 Chevy with the hood up. I kept expecting them to say you needed an oil change." At least I wasn't the only one seeing that nightmare image.

The nurses were very supportive, talking to me and Bernie and Bev, and wiping Bernie's brow as he worked with me, getting our second child born. Their whole manner toward the doctors radiated disapproval, according to Bev. But they showed a lot of approval for Bernie, as he encouraged me and cursed the doctors.

Oh, yes, cursed them to their faces. "Open your eyes," he said to me with each contraction. "Breathe. Now push. Push harder! Push that @o/c#'& doctor's hands out of you." Later he helped me push, saying, "Yes! Push! Don't worry about that $*!#@. Push! Good! We'll come back later and kill the %0*@$." And the nurses wiped our brows and said the baby was coming. She was born more slowly, and was met with even more delight. We had a daughter and a son – a matched set!

While Bernie and Bev hugged me, our daughter was weighed and wrapped up. She turned her head to follow their voices, eyes tracking Bernie as he came to tell Lila Marie Klassen her name.

Bev helped the nurse and orderly to wrap me up and get me on a stretcher to take me to my room to rest. She didn't feel very useful.

Three years later I knew how she felt, being neither nurse nor doctor nor spouse, outside the centre circle as I waited outside the door of the room where she gave birth. I heard the baby's cry, and Bev's voice matching it in delight and tears. My own tears came, as murmurs of praise were audible through the door.

Soon her husband, Al, came out into the dim room where I waited. He hugged me, telling me she was perfect, a girl named Arwen. He went to make phone calls. When Bev was brought out, a nurse asked me, "You're waiting here? Are you family, then?"

"She's my friend," Bev said, and I was allowed to help her shift to a bed and wrap up warmly.

Friends don't have much role in birth, but sometimes there's some small attention or a word that comforts. What did I do for Bev's labour and delivery? Not much: far, far less than she did for mine. I have memories which she gave me; what she saw and heard when I couldn't see or hear or speak to say what she and Bernie said for me.

Falling in Love Again

My baby blinked blue eyes at me and looked up, clean and sweet and nice, little arms coming round my head as I kissed the round, full tummy wrapped in a flannel nightie. I knew I loved my baby, not just wanted it, *loved* it with complete ferocity. More than my hands, my voice, my life, I loved this baby.

My baby closed sleepy blue eyes after a late-night nursing. I wrapped the flannel blanket more snugly, felt a burp and a contented sigh. I knew I loved my baby, wanted it and would do anything for it. Anything I could do wouldn't be enough for this baby I loved.

That first memory comes from two weeks after the twins' birth, the second from when they were almost a month old. Bonding with newborns is something parents and hospitals are fashionably sensitive about at present, encouraging the mother to keep the newborn in her hospital room so they can bond in the first days. With a multiple birth or complications, the process of getting acquainted and getting to love these warm, wet, noisy rascals takes a little more time.

And while I was falling in love twice in a month, where was the man I already loved?

Bernie regards *Fine Woodworking* magazine as "pornography for woodworkers." He's the only man I've ever caught watching a Celine Dion video (the one where she's rolling around in her slip, on a bed and later a massive Gothic armchair) while he's murmuring "No, no, no, – go back to the chair."

He was holding the babies in the nursery the morning after they were born, when the doctor came in to tell him I'd just hemorrhaged again and was back in Surgery. He rocked the babies, fed them and was promptly spat up upon, scared and sure in his heart that I was dying. (Even though ten units of blood and plasma went into me during the delivery and surgery, I was chalk white for weeks.) If I needed to take weeks to learn to love our children, that was fine with him, it seemed, just so long as he had me around at all.

So I had lots of encouragement to take my time learning how to care for the twins. That's "care for" as in looking after these pink wigglers with suction-cup mouths as well as coming to have tender feelings about them. It took a lot of practice before I was able to wrap the babies up as neatly as the nurses did, or my mother. I really tried, though, even in hospital when I finally woke up enough after fading in and out for three days.

Bernie and I learned how to change diapers, and we unwrapped the pink-and-white babies to count their toes, of course. Holding one or the other against his chest, Bernie sang to them the songs he had sung cuddled along my belly when they were growing, but what made me feel close to them again was nursing them.

My mother encouraged me to try, and boasted proudly to all the relatives and friends that I was "actually nursing both of them – at once!" It wasn't easy the first few times. I hit the alarm button for the nurse once when Ben choked and there was milk everywhere – mouth, nose, ears, and eyes. The panic was soon over and we learned to do this together, me hugging and burping the babies, and them sucking for all they were worth.

One morning at home I fell asleep with them and when I woke up an hour later they had drained me dry. It looked like I had two empty gym socks on my chest, with walnuts in the toes. Of course, that much drinking made my body think I'd actually had *quintuplets,* so the next morning my milk came in with a vengeance. I was standing full and spilling by their crib, poking into the bassinettes, saying "Wake up, babies. Aren't you hungry? Please wake up now!"

So there were times when it was uncomfortable, but there has never been anything as comforting for me as nursing. I felt so connected to the babies, and able to do what they needed so much more easily than wash bottles or clothes or wrestle the baby carriage out for a walk. When in doubt, nurse!

Nursing never felt wrong once in eight months – I did get some stares later, at gatherings, but Bernie and my friends treated nursing as normal. It felt loving, and it was connecting in a way that I wish everyone could feel at least once. Wouldn't the world be a better place if that could happen?

It took time to learn how to care for my twins, and time to learn how I loved them, and the people who love me gave me time to do this learning.

Outnumbered!

Something was obvious about having twins. I was outnumbered – right from the start!

It wasn't just the tag-team wailing or the diaper-change assembly line that convinced me. One baby would be comfortable and cuddly, or starting to fall asleep, while the other would be spitting up or messing another diaper and ready to boogie. I was eventually able to unbundle, clean, powder and cream a baby and wrap it up at two am with eyes shut. "Okay, Lila, here you go, sweetie... off with the wet diaper and – sorry, Ben, I didn't know it was you!"

I was even outnumbered by my nursing equipment. In fact, I needed a production team to assist with set-up for nursing sessions. There were three pillows, two babies and wiping cloths to get ready every time. (Breast shields, nipple protectors and breast pumps were really essential the few times they were needed.) Once a glass of water and the phone were put within reach, the pillows arranged, and babies handed to me one at a time, the effort to get the hungry little mouths latched on could begin.

It was easier nursing them both at once. My aunt gave me this great book, *Twins,* by Dr. Gillian Leigh, and it showed three positions for nursing twins. The photos made me giggle. Dr. Leigh recommends trying the first few times in bed, with lots of pillows and a helper to arrange cushions and hand the babies over, one at a time. I felt like a Queen Bee being groomed by workers.

One morning when we'd been doing this for about a week, I got Lila hooked up before turning to Ben, who was squalling with hunger. Turned out it wasn't only hunger, as my milk had let down and was spraying into his face. His little eyes and nose were full. No wonder he was complaining!

Burping at the half-way point, and after the feeding, worked easiest with an assistant burping at least one of the twins. And then the whole thing had to be done over again in another three hours.

People asked me if it was hard to get the twins on a schedule, or to keep them on the same schedule. Heck, I didn't know! I just started when they woke up, fed them, washed them, changed them, dressed them, rushed out of the nursery to feed and dress myself – and then it was time to start all over again. Later, when they went on a four-hour schedule, it was easier to do other things like wash dishes with the phone tucked under one ear, or fold laundry while watching *Star Trek* reruns. If it weren't for the television, I'd never have folded laundry. And ironing just didn't happen.

But when they got older, that was when it became very clear that there was one of me and two of them and it would take all the running around I could muster just to keep them both in sight at the same time.

The nursery was a safe place for the babies to crawl around. If I dumped a few plastic toys and a stuffed animal or two on the floor, the eight-month-old crawlers would explore them happily and I could leave the door open to the kitchen where I was making lunch or drinking a cup of tea.

One morning I set them up, went into the kitchen, and washed one dinner plate. One! Then my "parent radar" went off and I began to worry. But what could babies get into?

They'd managed to get the lid off a new five hundred millilitre jar of Vaseline. Baby-scented. It was smeared all over their sleepers, and in a six-foot wide circle around the spot where they were sitting, handing the plastic jar back and forth so they could take turns eating greasy handfuls.

When my voice would work again, I shrieked, "What are you doing?" Both babies started and dove their fists into the jar for one more handful which they crammed in their mouths before crawling away in opposite directions. They couldn't have done better if they'd planned it.

They didn't get very far - the greasy floor meant they were crawling-on-the-spot instead of making a clean get-away. By the time I caught and, more importantly, hung onto them both, I was laughing too hard to be upset. The Poison Control Hotline agreed with the jar label that Vaseline was not harmful to eat, though it might be a "mild laxative." We peeled off all the Vaseline-ed clothes and had a bath in the big tub. It made a great story to tell Bernie.

He had his own ending for the story the next morning, though, when he was busy on the diaper-change assembly line. Those diapers – full of Vaseline which had gone through the kids – were unbelievably foul. These were the only cloth diapers that we treated as disposables. It was a lot easier to take the trash out that morning, too, with one of us handling the chore and the other handling the kids.

Two adults can outnumber two kids anytime ... at least as long as they're babies.

How Do I Look From Behind?

There's a photograph in our album. The babies are slumped over, asleep in their two folding strollers which Bernie has clamped together, and I am smiling, pushing them up a slight hill past the cement yard near our home. They are flushed and rosy in their sunhats; in the July heat I am wearing shorts.

"Wow!" says my daughter, looking at the picture eight years later. "I never saw you so skinny!"

As easy as that, the picture changes. What had been a photo of my pride and joy (yes, people use cliches like that when we become parents) in my two healthy babies and my strength to be able to take care of them and show them off on that sunny day, is now seen differently. Were my shorts too short, my grin too vacuous? Did I look empty-headed, like a mother with a one-track mind? From eight years' distance, I can look at that photo and think, "At least I was slimmer then, and I look happy."

From behind the stroller, it was a different day. I was happy to see the person who took the photograph – my neighbour Erna who often came for tea, and babysat one evening, while Bernie read at his first poetry reading. It was nice to see Erna after walking to Chinatown for fortune cookies. The weather was warm for the first day in a long while. It was a good day.

It was a good day in contrast to a not-so-good night, where I had been up to nurse the twins twice and hadn't slept between the feedings. There had been the tiredness that doesn't lead to sleep, and the tears that don't change anything.

It was a good day after days of rain, short walks and no one to meet when I did bundle the twins up and go out. It was a good day after three weeks in which not one person talked to me except for my husband, my mother and my doctor. I kept track.

Were friends giving me "space" to bond with my kids? Was I invisible to people walking past me on the sidewalk? I couldn't tell.

Looking through the photo album, it is so good to see myself at happy moments like this walk, coming up the hill and seeing Erna. It helps me remember now, the time of colic and cracked nipples wasn't all just nights when I couldn't sleep at eleven-thirty, and mornings when I got the house tidied up by nine am, but no one came over.

It doesn't show in the photo that I was bone-tired and becoming depressed, but it showed to some people. My mother bought diaper service for four months. My father came over one morning on his way to work.

"I hear the babies have colic," he said. "I don't know what to do for colic. But upset mothers make upset babies, so I brought this for you to relax." He put a portable TV set on the bookshelf. "It's only an old black and white, but you can get two or three channels even without cable. You can watch it in the evenings when you're cuddling them. When you're relaxed, maybe they will feel better, too."

His idea worked at least as well as any colic remedy I ever heard. Watching old Star Trek reruns while folding diapers was a quiet way to wind down before bed. It slowed down the late-night thinking, too, but it didn't stop it.

What if the babies stop breathing in the night? What if I drop a babe? What if the reason I'm so tired is that I'm going to die?

Today, eight years of listening to the kids breathing at night makes some of these fears seem pretty unreal. But I had heard each of them draw their first breaths. They seemed so fragile, especially when they were eight months old and so sick with colds that they couldn't keep anything down. After three days they started getting better, and we cuddled with their bottles on the couch, reading stories or watching TV for half an hour before bed. The French channel came in clearly sometimes, and I watched it occasionally, trying not to lose the language. I had finished a University degree in French and Creative Writing, and took an extra ten months to get a teaching certificate, but got pregnant a month before the practicum year ended. The nice new teaching certificate seemed like it would never get used; certainly not while there were diapers to wash and this horrible tiredness!

It didn't help that people were no longer treating me like a sensible adult. Oh, some friends and most women strangers were fine. But store clerks, the property manager, or business people – when they didn't ignore me! – talked like I couldn't put two thoughts together in my head.

One night I stood in the hallway where the typewriter and desk stood next to the stroller and diaper bag, and looked wistfully at my old text books. Our bookshelves towered eight feet high: over forty feet of shelving loaded with books. That was just the "study." The living room and kitchen had two more bookshelves. So did the bathroom, bedroom and nursery.

"I am a poet!" I shrieked. "I am an academic! I am a teacher! I am a trained professional! I just finished writing a novel! What does all this baby stuff have to do with me? Why do I get treated like the baby?"

When I caught my breath I went to wring out the wet laundry and put it in the dryer. The kids were wearing my t-shirts because all their bunny sleepers were in the wash. Even novelists and academics have to do the laundry sometimes.

It was time to do something about this depression and fatigue which were building till I felt ready to die. When I looked up Mental Health in the phone book, there was the listing. And the address was... the Institute. The big building just off a main street, with doors that locked tight and windows that wouldn't open.

"Rah rah, root root, We're from the Institute. It's fun to be a Men...tal." The kids I used to teach at a suburban playground sang this chant when someone missed a ball. Once I went to the Institute to visit a friend with innumerable tiny slices between her elbow and wrist. Another friend had anorexia counselling there. She weighed eighty-seven pounds and jogged a lot.

The Lamaze classes which Bernie and I had taken before the twins were born were held in the Institute. While, on the one hand, holding Lamaze classes in the Institute might suggest that having kids would make anyone crazy, on the other hand, it did reassure me that not everybody who went to the Institute got locked up in a rubber room. So I bundled up my courage and went there.

The door was locked. Nobody was there. They were all away for two hours for lunch. I cried all over Bernie and the babies, buckled into their "baby buckets" in the truck we had borrowed from my dad. I'd have to come back another day.

I did come back. And I filled out their forms so I could have free counselling because I couldn't afford even the bus fare to get to the appointments most days. And Bernie came with me.

Our friend Garth babysat every Thursday for most of a year. At first we had to reassure him. "If we come home to find the house in flames but you're on the front lawn with the toddlers in your arms, you win." He became confident at playing blocks.

Meanwhile, we learned about post-natal depression and manic-depressive syndrome. It seems that most mothers have the "baby blues" for a short while; and many mothers find themselves in a depression severe enough to seek advice from their doctors as well as family and friends. (Most of us feel better when the kids grow up and move out.) Medication or intense therapy is rarely needed, and the most effective relief seems to come from talking with other parents and adults. (Getting enough sleep, good nutrition and support from a loving family work wonders, too!)

We learned that manic-depressive syndrome is linked to a gene more common among Eastern European people, including Mennonites and Hutterites. People who are manic-depressive are often highly intelligent and creative. Some take medication for a short while, or on a long-term basis, to help keep their energetic moods on an even keel or pull them out of depression phases. In addition, we learned about talking without having to solve problems all at once. We learned ways to express grieving.

It became clear that, whatever else was happening to each of us, giving birth with the help of an obstetrician who never addressed a word to me, once labour began, had been traumatic for both Bernie and I. Even as Bernie gave me encouragement, and he and our friend Bev helped me through labour and delivery, Bernie had been terrified that I would die, both then and the morning after when I hemorrhaged. It took months after the birth for me to get stronger; even today, several years later, I still feel as though a third of my strength and endurance is gone.

As my health continued to improve, and we learned to talk with each other and our counsellors, other things began to get better. Living apart for a year gave Bernie and me space to enjoy our time together and with our kids. The babies grew into bright, active toddlers. Our families were helpful with presents and babysitting.

When it seemed like every day of the week was the same, I joined a parents' group which met Wednesday mornings, giving me time out from the twins. Talking together, we parents were astonished at how such different people could have so many similar things happen to them. Later I ran a writers' workshop and volunteered on a community paper and hosted poetry readings with people who became friends.

Bernie changed jobs, working the night audit at a somewhat nicer hotel than before. The police didn't have to be called out as often to this hotel. When a drunk staggered up to Bernie's counter, saying, "Would ya call me a taxi?" Bernie would smile.

(This was the part of the job he liked best, next to the typewriter which he used to write letters to his Texan penpal at four in the morning.) "Certainly," Bernie would say. "You, sir, are a taxi." Then he'd dial the number and hand the phone to the puzzled drunk.

Sometimes I look back on those days, particularly the days when I began feeling well again, and I'm not sure what marked each small improvement. Was it getting more sleep? Selling a story for (gasp) money? Writing a short novel on Labour Day Weekend for The Three-Day Novel Contest? Starting a writers' workshop so that I could use my degree to teach and learn with people? Or maybe it was that the children were growing older and were so bright and healthy, earning me praise from the people who helped me raise them. I feel like the woman in the Stan Rogers song who looks into the mirror at the lines in her face that must be telling lies. "Then she shakes off the bitter web she wove... And she thinks ahead to Friday, 'cause Friday will be fine."

Even now, everything isn't perfect. But any one day is usually fine. I can look in the mirror and feel pretty good about what I see, lines in the face, plump figure and all. But how do I look from behind? The mirror doesn't show. Sometimes I have to look in the photo album to get hindsight.

A One-Man Committee

When Bernie is doing anything, he's busy enough to be a one-man committee. This is not a 24-hour-a-day quality, because he does take time off. Nobody can read two papers while eating a box of Alpha-Bits cereal with a pint of cream like he can. And does, once in a while. But when he's working on one of his projects, he keeps busy enough for a whole work crew. And if anyone asks him what he's been doing or reading or planning lately, he can talk about it with the intensity of a television preacher and the charm of a carnival barker.

These projects can be anything from a new design for a black walnut china cabinet to articles for the small press science fiction magazine he edited for a few years. He can discuss everything from the European history of the block plane to ethical population control, and afterward you don't even feel like there's going to be a test on Friday.

When it comes to the practical application of his knowledge, Bernie sometimes drinks a couple of pots of coffee while deciding what he's going to do. But usually he has the situation all planned out long beforehand, and when it's time, he does exactly what he set out to do. Or, if a decision involves both of us, we plan it out together.

Such as the birth control issue. Before the twins were born, we had both been responsible for birth control. Keeping track of my fertile times and using diaphragms and condoms had certainly been an interesting hobby, but forgetting my cervical cap *just one time* had been enough to make us parents of twins. We seemed to be fertile enough that another lapse of memory like the first might make us parents of triplets, and we didn't feel ready for that.

We had researched the whole issue of birth control, and in Bernie's mind, the answer was for him to get a vasectomy. I agreed, and one fine morning when the twins were three months old, he hopped on the bus headed to the hospital for his scheduled vasectomy. It wouldn't take long, and he could come home a couple of hours after waking up from the anaesthetic.

That's right, the same hospital that did not knock me out when I delivered twins used a general anaesthetic for vasectomies. "With the older guys, I sometimes give them a mirror so they can watch," the doctor told Bernie. "But you young guys tend to get a little distressed, so I like to put you under."

Distressed? Bernie was cracking jokes! While the orderly was shaving him for surgery, the doctor came in to see if Bernie was ready and had any questions. Nope, everything was fine, until Bernie called out, "No, wait Doc, you gotta tell me – this has really been bugging me, and I wanna know – does this mean I get fat and sleep on top of the television set a lot?"

The orderly laughed at the line, too, and Bernie nearly had his vasectomy on the spot.

When he woke after the operation with a nurse telling him everything was fine, Bernie found an icepack on his lap. "It's to reduce swelling," the nurse said. Bernie is never too sleepy to joke around.

"What are ya trying to do, increase my fertility? I just had a vasectomy!" (Cold packs and loose boxer shorts are recommended for men trying to increase their sperm counts, as the nurse was well aware.)

He had a wisecrack for everyone in Post-Op. After an hour of this, the nurse asked who was supposed to be picking him up, and he gave them our home number.

When she called, I'd been having a rather different sort of day at home. Since Bernie had caught the bus, I'd nursed the three-month-old twins twice and given them baths. My brother, Karl, had agreed to pick Bernie up at the hospital, and he came over to wait for the phone call announcing that Bernie was ready to leave. Of course, I immediately enlisted Karl as assistant baby-burper and diaper-changer. He spent a busy hour learning how much fluid goes in and out of babies.

"Putting Ben into these little sleepers," Karl said, closing tiny snaps with his big hands, "is like putting a banana back into its peel." Lila was still burping on my shoulder when the phone rang again, as it had been ringing all day with carpet cleaner salesmen. I'd had about enough phone calls interrupting the diaper-change assembly line, so I answered it by saying, "Paula's baby factory."

There was a moment's silence on the line, then the nurse said, "This certainly has to be the right number. I'm calling for Bernie Klassen. Are you ready to come and get him at the hospital?" I could hear Bernie's voice in the background, calling out, "Hi, Beautiful!"

I was surprised. "Yes, his ride can come and get him, but are you sure he's ready? He was supposed to wait there for another hour."

"Ready?" snorted the nurse. "He's been in Post-Op for the last hour, telling jokes to everybody when they come out of surgery. He's fine. Get him out of here!"

Just how popular Bernie was among the appendectomy and hernia patients, I'm not sure. But Karl brought Bernie home, smiling and sleepy and still cracking jokes. Since then, he's been a one-man advocacy committee for vasectomies, and spreads the good word about them to friends who think long-term birth control is a woman's concern. His bawdy good humour is interwoven with comments like: "Really, it's no big deal and you never have to worry about it again."

His advocacy campaign is pretty effective, as several of his friends have joined the committee of "Men Who Think Vasectomies Are Really Cool." But you can't tell who they are just by looking at them talking around a table; you have to listen to what they say – and I don't mean the pitch of their voice. Not all of them are comedians like Bernie or as bawdy, but comments ranging from "Yep! I'm shooting blanks now," to "If we ever do want more kids, we'll adopt," are good clues as to who has joined the club.

I Working!

Somewhere along the way from babies to toddlers, both twins picked up the idea that (drum roll) ... it's FUN to be busy! Maybe they figured Mommy must be having fun when she's busy, otherwise she'd stop making dinner and get right back to jiggling babies.

They liked a good jiggle. When they were still small enough to wrap up in flannel blankets, I'd bundle them like footballs and set them up in a baby carriage in the big kitchen. Jiggle it, and the springs would keep it rocking while I peeled potatoes; jiggle jiggle – stir the soup; jiggle jiggle – set the table.

When the twins were six months old and sitting up, this didn't work as well, so I'd put them on the floor of their room and they'd get busy with a toy. Sometimes a muffled banging from the basement would echo through the nursery as Bernie beat up wood or his thumb, eventually emerging with an end table or bookshelf. "Mama!" They would be baffled. They could hear him but not see him – and I would explain, "Daddy's working. Hear his hammer banging?" How much was understood by two kids who had a working vocabulary of three words, I don't know.

The only real words they could say at that point, after a great deal of coaching, were Ma-ma, MA-ma (for Grandma) and Da! They learned Ma-ma early, and used it only for the people who looked after them. Bernie was taken aback at being called Ma-ma, and several times would be found with one or both babies on his lap saying, "Da-da. I'm Da-da. Da. Da. Say Da-da!" The first "Da!" delighted everyone, (Bernie in particular), but after that they were back to nonsense sounds like "golly-golly-golly" and "boodla-boodla-boodla." It seemed they weren't working on talking until months later when all kinds of words came pouring out in a sudden torrent.

Then a short step to short sentences. "Da-da working!" when they heard thumping from the basement workshop. "Kiss Mama" was for when I had a headache and would get right down for them to kiss my forehead and make it all better. And boy, did they get busy.

They imitated us. If I stirred up something in a mixing bowl, they got pots and whanged spoons around inside them. Making bread meant a lot of pestering from the tots until each got a small lump of dough to knead. The crooked bread shapes they made were baked and admired, but not always eaten. When Bernie picked up the coffeepot and sugar bowl after friends came over, Ben or Lila would pick up a coffee cup and carry it, sloshing cold coffee, all the way to the sink. "I working," said with six teeth and a smile.

One morning, a TV puppet show had a little song about people working at different jobs. We let the year-old toddlers watch and sing along – mostly singing Ya-ya-ya – and took the weekend paper and big mugs of tea to bed. (I know, I know. Who needs *The Globe and Mail* when there's a Real Man in her bed? But marital intimacy takes many forms. Trust me.)

We left the door open and could hear the twins singing and clapping hands to the music, smacking the futon couch, tapping on something or other... "What are you doing, Ben?" Bernie asked as he went through the living room to the kitchen.

"I working, Da-dee!" came Ben's cheerful call. Working? At what? I wondered, still in the paper. Bernie squawked. I left our warm nest to look in the next room. Our two angels were still bouncing and singing along with the TV puppets, but facing the wall above the futon couch – where Ben was very busy indeed. He had an egg whisk clutched in his chubby fist, and was using the narrow end to pry pieces of plaster out of the wall. He had made quite a hole, too – about a square foot – in those few moments.

Oh, horrors! In distress we explained, very clearly and carefully, that it was a marvelous job, but we really didn't need any more holes in the wall. "But I working, Da-dee!" Ben cried. Bitter tears followed from Lila. She wanted to poke her own hole in the wall.

This mess meant Bernie had to mix Poly-filla and repair the wall, of course, which appeared to have been badly repaired when an earlier tenant of this old house had fixed a crack from the home settling over the years.

But before that, Bernie made a pounding toy called a "cobbler's bench." Similar to the much frailer and more expensive version sold in toy stores, this gizmo had an old switch or two on the ends, as well as sturdy pegs to pound in from one side, flip over, and pound back.

This toy never broke under three years of pounding. The kids jumped onto it out of their playhouse. They stood it on end to boost them up to the cookie jar on the pantry cupboard. When we moved, we gave it to another kid who didn't have a hammer, but cheerfully pounded away with a rock. It was most popular when Bernie was down in his shop, running a power tool or hammering; one or both twins would sit on the kitchen floor which was vibrating like a drum from the sound of the table saw, hold the cobbler's bench between small feet, and pound away. "I working!" was their chant, from one to three years old.

This could be a good chant. It could also bring Bernie running with a wet paintbrush, or get me to leave the wringer washer wringing a towel in a perpetual loop, to see exactly what our busy workers were working on.

"What are you doing, Lilly-billy?"

"I working, Mama." The cobbler's bench? No problem. Washing the dishes I had left soaking in the sink? Big problem.

"I wuz helping you wash da gyasses, but I can't get 'em apawt," Lila admitted. The two glasses had broken when she tried to twist them apart. Her guardian angel was busy that day keeping her away from the sharp edges! I put the rest of the glasses in boxes with our Royal Albert china from the wedding. So what if we drank milk or juice from coffee mugs? No more broken glass!

"Monday's child is fair of face, Tuesday's child is full of grace." Ben and Lila were born on a Saturday, and "Saturday's child works hard for a living." They're certainly living up to it so far, and it's a lot of work keeping up with them.

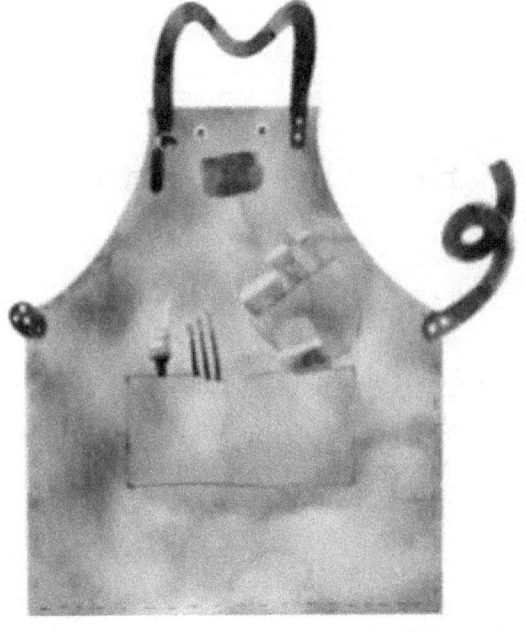

How Did You Know?

The moment I fell asleep, the babies woke up.

And if I even thought about making love, wails would come from the nursery. At six months old, it was usually Lila who woke her brother. She woke up even if I had a nightmare. I tried patting and soothing her back to sleep. "Shhh, Lily, that was Mama's dream, not yours. Go back to sleep, sweetie." It worked as well as anything else.

WHEN BEN WAS JUST LEARNING to walk, he had night terrors, waking up screaming. Bernie could hold him up clear off the crib and his little legs would still be running, his arms flailing. He'd wake up, cry and be soothed back to sleep. After the third or fourth dream like this, he had learned to talk well enough to say he'd had a dream. "It's all gone now," Bernie told him.

"How you know, Dada?"

"Because I'm the Dad. I know." He had no more night terrors after that.

I CAUGHT EIGHTEEN-MONTH-old Ben outside the back door, spitting out half a caterpillar. "Ben! Bugs are not food! They're yucky!"

He nodded, eyes wide. "How you know, Mama?"

LILA LOVED TO DRESS up. One day, this two-year-old pulled off her clothes, reached into my clean laundry, put on a short, lacy camisole, and snugged two knee-high nylons up to her hips. "Aren't I pretty, Mama?" she asked, standing with one knee flexed.

Personally, I thought she looked like she had a promising career in exotic dance ahead of her. Aloud I said only, "The prettiest little girl I know!"

She smiled like a semi-nude angel. "Now I gonna dance!"

AT TWO YEARS OLD, LILA began waking up, crying, some nights. Soothing didn't quiet her as she threw tantrums: heels drumming on floor, hitting and crying. Talking, leaving her in bed, light on, light off: nothing helped. She stormed and raged, quieting gradually after an hour of being held so that she didn't bang her head.

After a couple of nights I was ready to do a little wailing and banging myself. I made a cup of tea, trying not to cry while she cried on the floor at my feet. I turned on the dusty TV set, found a late-night movie, and sat on the couch beside her. More wails. But the sobs did run down, and her trembling stopped. She fell asleep.

The next time it happened, a week later, as soon as she went rigid in my arms, I laid her on the couch, turned on the late movie and made popcorn. She calmed down after about fifteen minutes and we shared the wee-hours-of-the-morning snack.

The next morning, I said when she woke up, "Wasn't that a nice time we had, sitting on the couch after you stopped crying? Would you like to do that again? Well, next time you don't have to cry. If you ever wake up, we'll just make the snack and have a nice story or movie without all that awful crying, okay?"

Two nights later, it happened again. "Remember our plan?"

She was starting to drum her heels and howl when the sound of popcorn drifted out of the kitchen. "Oh yeah." We watched part of an old Danny Kaye movie, and she went back to bed, happy as a clam.

I told her grandparents, in case it ever happens when they're babysitting. But these night crying spells happened only about once a year after that – I still don't know why.

Making Friends

When Bernie and I lived apart for a while, it wasn't easy for either of us. It wasn't any easier for our friends and family to understand – nobody was quite sure whether this meant divorce papers would soon be served. Nobody, that is, but Bernie and me.

Maybe it didn't seem realistic, expecting to get our heads straight and live together again. It worked out pretty well from the start, though, particularly with Bernie taking time with the kids. I knew from the day after Bernie moved out that we were still able to work together, especially as a family.

Bernie came over that afternoon (over, not home... funny how conscious I was of that distinction) and we ate pears with the eighteen-month-old twins. Ben gobbled his pear, taking bite after bite, swallowing without chewing. Suddenly he choked. His face turned red, then black, as Bernie picked him up and laid him across his knee.

Bernie cleared the chunks of pear from Ben's mouth, and just as I was about to call 911, Ben was able to breathe again. He howled. He scrambled off Bernie's knee, and stumbled over to me, upset.

Daddy had taken his pear away, and he wanted it back!

We hugged him and tried to calm him. His breathing whistled as he cried. This did not bode well. We put him and Lila in their cribs for quiet time, gave them their bottles, and listened to the whistling while we called the hospital. A friend drove Bernie and Ben to the hospital, where a doctor agreed with our suspicion that Ben had a piece of pear caught in his lung.

Our teamwork that had come into play as Ben choked kept on working. Bernie stayed with Ben, who had a brachioscopy that evening and stayed the night for observation. Ben was none the worse the next day for having a tube put down his throat, complete with camera and tiny grabber to pick up the pear. Bernie was all the better for being the one to be there for Ben, instead of being shut out of the family.

Ben was completely well after an incident that would have been very troublesome before brachioscopes were invented. The lasting effect of that day was that it became really clear that no matter what, Bernie and I could work together to take care of the kids. Even in a worst-case scenario, if we didn't ever live together again, we knew we were still a team and we'd still be able to work together to do and be what our kids needed from us.

It was confusing, working around Bernie's schedule on the graveyard shift, night auditing for a hotel. It was pretty comical, too, visiting with – almost dating! – my husband. But we pulled it together, a little at a time. We started with the pears. No more hard pears! I put them aside for a while, until they ripened, and were ready.

How We Learn to Talk

My little niece is learning to talk at sixteen months. Mostly she says, "Hi!" at the top of her voice, and crows, "Cat!" with delight whenever one of the cats slinks past her stroller. I have it on good authority that she also says "Mama" "Da" and "dog" but she never does it when I'm around.

My friend, Linda's, daughter is the same age, and babbles a mile a minute. Whenever I phone their house, the toddler's voice is going up and down in the background, a sing-song of nonsense stringing together the odd real word. (Odd is right. The kid's been on so many camping canoe trips, her next word will probably be "portage.")

Both these little girls babble. But my friend Kris' son hardly spoke, and only to her. She read books about it, and asked her doctor. There didn't seem to be any hearing impairment, and the little guy understood what was said to him, so Kris decided to do what the doctor and one of the books suggested: wait until he's two years old before panicking and making appointments with specialists. As she might have guessed, Kris found that one month before his second birthday, her son began speaking to almost everyone he met – in short sentences, no less! He had just learned to speak in a different way, like Einstein and Thomas Carlisle.

Now Kris, Linda, and my sister-in-law have all learned to speak in a different way, too – they're talking like parents. It's terrific to listen to them when they turn from talking to me on the phone to telling a little one to quit pulling on Mommy's hair. Their tones of voice change three or four times, as they register pain, react, and realise that I can hear every word they say to the little one, who may still have a grip on Mommy's hair.

It's not only the tones of voice that change, but the vocabulary. I couldn't get over hearing a businesswoman friend ask her crawling baby if he wanted his "soose." Baby talk? From this flawlessly-groomed professional? Only later, when she took something from his clenched fist, saying "*Touche pas*," did I realize she was using French. A "pacifier" is "*la suce*" en francais.

"Pardon my French" works in other ways, too. While Bernie has inadvertently taught our children that "some words are for when Daddy drops the hammer on his foot", I, too, have had to check that my vocabulary is appropriate. After all, I never want to repeat my mother's discovery that if she burned herself at the stove and said something in reaction, the baby would repeat the word until Grandma came to visit.

These changes in my choice of words were small, but even today they still give a certain "kid-oriented" tone to my speech. What really surprises me is that my friends and co-workers start picking up these words, too, so that now all the radish-pickers on the farm are saying, "Don't pick the scootzy little ones." Okay, so we don't sound like geniuses. We get the point across!

This choice of "kid-oriented" words rather than standard ones may explain why parents of small children are sometimes treated like they have lost all their marbles. When we learn to talk with our kids, do we forget how to talk with other people? A sociologist friend once explained sympathetically to me that she had read a documented study which said that women permanently lose ten IQ points when they have children.

Oh yeah? is my response. IQ tests are biased, and only measure how well people can do IQ tests, anyway. When tests are used to tell people they're stupid and can't learn, the tests are part of the problem. I'll bet the women in that study didn't do as well on the tests after they became mothers because they were busy planning schedules, balancing budgets, and figuring out how much work they could get done while the kids were asleep. Marking little boxes on test papers just isn't a high priority compared with juggling food allergies, babysitters, and the learning needs of active children.

So, like my friend Kris, with the boy who learned to talk well, but later than the average kid, I'm not going to worry about living up to someone else's average score. My kids are talking well, and now I'm going to reclaim my own words after reading so many kids' books aloud at bedtime. It's not like the twins and I haven't always talked a lot every day, it's just that now I feel we've each got something to say.

Parents' Time Out

The notice in the paper said that a New Parents' Discussion Group was meeting at a community building called The Cove, so I bundled up the kids and trundled the twin stroller across several busy streets to find out what a Discussion Group was like. So did several other women. It turned out we were The Group that was just starting up, one that gave me a powerful sense of community, in a place where all my abilities became valued and useful.

Who were we strangers who had nothing in common? Nothing, that is, but the toddlers playing in a sunny room downstairs, watched over by pairs of twelve-year-old girls who took turns getting a morning off school. We all approved of the babysitting deal. These girls wouldn't have a baby at fifteen just because babies are soooo cute. These girls had changed diapers!

So what did we parents have in common besides experience changing diapers? One parent was a teenaged single mother. Another mother had a new baby and a sixteen-year-old. Three had husbands, the rest were divorced or single or separated. We lived in different parts of the city, came from different backgrounds, had different jobs, educations, interests and shoe sizes.

But boy, were we all tired! Tired of looking after our kids till it seemed like nobody else did it and we did nothing else. Tired of not being noticed by anybody except our kids, kids who did notice any tiny lapse of attention and, to prevent it happening again, would knock over the sugarbowl, barge into the bathroom or eat a jar of Zincofax ointment. Tired of late nights and long days and people saying, "It must be nice to be at home instead of working."

We talked about the easy things at first: who was still nursing, who wanted to go back to school or to a job, who knew the only grocery store in town that delivered. It took a few months of Wednesday mornings before one of us admitted she was afraid that, just by being on welfare, she was Social Services' idea of a bad mother, and half-way to having her kids taken away.

Six of the eight of us were on welfare, and admitted to the same fear. Our facilitator went to her social worker, asked the question for us, and came back with good news: children were taken only from parents who abused them or didn't take care of them. People on welfare usually took good care of their children, said the social worker. Funny how we had never read that in the newspaper! Talking about this and other news items led to some of us participating in an Anti-Poverty Conference two years later.

We didn't expect to share another fear. I described one day how I'd been walking with the baby carriage on a sidewalk above a low place, and a man walked toward me. The idea struck me then, and again in nightmares, that if he grabbed one of the babies and flung it over the edge, I would be unable to go after the one baby without leaving the other with a madman. Every bit of reluctance I felt describing this (would they say I was crazy? paranoid? a man-hater?) faded when I looked up to see ashen faces. Every one of them had the same fear, the same nightmare. And it was always about a man. Once we saw it as some sort of archetypal fear, it was easier to look at individual men and realize how few of them were in any way dangerous – and what to do about the few who were.

Other fears became problems we could do something about. One of us lobbied to have a crosswalk sign replaced. Another spoke out to her analyst when he gave her bad advice. We shared suggestions on how to discipline our kids. Time Out in a corner was really popular, but when Lila got into real tantrums, I'd occasionally have to sit down and hold her till she finished struggling. All of us parents had come this close to punting our offspring into the Harbour. What kept us from becoming another appalling statistic was mostly being able to take a break now and then, even if it was only one minute on the phone while the tot howled in the play pen.

Another child-saver was the resolution that we were the adults. It didn't matter if our little tyrants had IQs of 160 or special needs – Mom was the one who decided what would happen, when and how it would be done. It was a noble goal, even if it didn't always work the first time the way it was planned.

"How do you get your groceries with a twin stroller?" Carol asked me one Wednesday meeting.

"I used to push the stroller and pull the cart." I mimed the action. "Now I put them each in a shopping cart, one pushed and one pulled."

"My kid fusses for candy and junk. He's worse than his big brother. It must be awful with two to kick up a fuss."

The twins had tried that, once. Everyone wanted to know what I'd done, so I admitted that I'd left the store and gone home. "Dinner that night was peanut butter and crackers. When they said, 'Mama, this isn't very much like dinner,' I told them that we had been buying dinner when they kicked up a fuss, pestering for treats. Boy, where they sorry. After that, no problem."

Carol's jaw dropped. "What am I doing, buying groceries when my sixteen-year-old has just got his driver's licence? Next time I'm giving him a list and he can see how much money is left for pop!"

Some of us were so shy that it was clear we needed to get out and talk with people more. Those of us accustomed to whirlwind social activity were starving for it. Talking together once a week was great, but we wanted more.

We began having a monthly Family Potluck Dinner in The Cove. Eating at restaurants cost too much, eating at someone's house meant making it spiffy-clean for guests (nobody was up for that,) and eating at McDonald's meant keeping the kids quiet in a packed room of busy strangers. Potluck dinners were better: we had time and space to talk out loud, the kids could play, and sometimes we shared a video or a game. Some husbands and friends came.

I liked these programs so much, I spoke with our facilitator about volunteering to help with more. She needed help from any warm body! Before long I was writing for the monthly newspaper, helping with fairs, and facilitating a writers' workshop. The three-year-old twins went to a daycare a block away with some kids from the Parents' Time Out, and they loved it. Any time this felt like a hassle, I compared it with people stuck in 8-to-4 jobs who couldn't work the evening at a monthly poetry reading, then take a morning off to talk and play with only one of the twins.

One day I did that with Lila, and walked to a park we'd never seen before. All the way back, she sang, "Twelve sticky buns in a bakery shop, Big and round with currants on the top. Along came a little girl and took one away. Eleven sticky buns in the shop today!"

Another time it was Ben's turn to explore a weeping birch and teach me a different song. "Down by the bay, where the watermelons grow, back to my home I dare not go. For if I do, my mother would say, 'Did you ever see an elephant doing something irrelevant, down by the bay?"' I learned they liked to play horse shoes, and to have Mommy "all to myself with nobody else!"

They liked daycare so much that I applied for a government grant for The Cove, and got a job there. There was even paid work for another person for most of that year. We set up a Farmer's Market, an Arts Festival, and got even more active in the community. We still kept the basics going strong, though – the writers' workshop, poetry readings, neighbourhood festivals and, of course, the Parents' Time Out.

When the grant was finished, I reviewed my assets, and there were a few new ones on the list. The stories and poems I was writing were better than anything I'd done before, for one. I was confident enough to teach for a few months, and to work as a Recreation Programmer for a few months when we moved to Alberta. But I kept writing, and selling a story or a poem here, a book review or an article there, until one day, four years later, it became clear that I had worn out the printer of my second-hand computer. I wasn't just someone who loved writing; I was a writer who needed a new word processor and could buy one with money earned from writing. Where does encouragement end and confidence begin? I'm not there yet, but I'm on my way.

Yakkity Yak – Don't Talk Back!

How did it feel, arriving at "woman's estate" in the full flower of my powers, with two beautiful, smart children to show for it? Lousy. The only people who held doors open for me when I was pregnant or pushing strollers were pregnant women pushing strollers. I knew the location of every public restroom (all four) in downtown Victoria and every curb too high to navigate with a baby buggy. And if society was supposedly organized to protect women and children, how come it took a Gold Credit Card to get any attention in department stores?

It all came to a head at a party one night in my parents' home. My two-year-old daughter was talking to a guest and twisting her own little plaid skirt in one fist.

Another guest nudged me. "That your little girl? Boy, you're gonna have a lot of trouble with that one when she's sixteen!"

"Well, she's two going on sixteen right now," I shrugged.

His bald spot shone as he shook his head. "Naw, I mean she's gonna be flipping her skirt up like that, she's gonna be giving you a lot of trouble with the boys."

I couldn't believe this was supposed to be a co-worker of my mother's. What a creep! I tried to remember some of the non-aggressive statements they'd talked about in Parenting Classes. "I don't like what you said. You hurt my feelings talking about my daughter like that – "

"Too bad," said the creep with the bald spot. "You can't stop people saying things when she sashays around like that."

I bit back a four-letter word. He wasn't really a symbol of every so-and-so who crowded my stroller in doorways, who wouldn't give up his bus seat when

I was pregnant or who honked his car horn when I walked two two-year-olds across a road. Maybe he was just a creep who didn't think how he hurt my feelings. I decided to hold back from stomping on his feelings, and managed a non-aggressive smile, and even an old corn-pone joke to defuse the situation. "If you're so damned smart, why ain't you rich?"

"But I am!" He laughed – the deep, confident laugh that invited all within earshot to laugh with him. "I'm fabulously rich!"

Bingo. No reason to hold back now. "Ten bucks." I held out my hand.

"What?" No one was laughing with him, but he didn't notice.

"Gimme ten bucks and I'll listen to anything you have to say."

His jowls flapped. "I'm not giving you ten dollars!"

"And *I'm* not listening to anything *you* have to say. *Quit saying filthy things about my kid*," I hissed in a voice that would blister paint.

He muttered something that sounded exactly like, "Fussy witch." The deep, confident laugh rang a little hollow when he got his coat and said good-bye to my parents, who were busy with a crowd of relatives, friends and co-workers. I hear he was a high-level civil servant, who lost his job in cutbacks soon after that. (And they say there is no justice in the world...)

There is some justice in the world, I know, or at the very least, mercy. When I strollered into the bank that spring with both kids teething, tired and crying, there was a line of about twelve people waiting for the teller, and no bank machine.

"Excuse me," I said to the people lined up, who of course had noticed the twins' crying and were trying to ignore it politely. "But I think it might be easier for everyone ... if I could please go first ... instead of waiting?"

The same faces that had been carefully blank lit up in smiles. Of course they would let me go first! No one wanted to make me wait with the toddlers' voices echoing under that high ceiling. They could be generous, and thoughtful, and let me go first and get out of there quickly before the noise drove them bats!

I cashed a cheque in record time and said thank-you to all the nice, smiling, relieved people who had all done their good deed for the day. There are still neighbourly people out there, willing to be polite and friendly when given the chance, when I chance to find them.

How Many Times Did You Fall Down Today?

For years, I could always tell when my in-laws were coming to visit: one of the children would fall down and develop a spectacular bruise. A day or two later, when the child's leg or forehead was turning purple and yellow, the grandparents would arrive.

Never failed.

One time my son counted twenty-five "owies" and accounted for each one of them to me at bath time. "This one I got in the cherry tree, this one on the driveway, playing ball, I fell down, Neil hit me, my new book gave me a paper cut, (on his nose?) I stubbed my toe ..." I daubed him with Bactine, checked my daughter's Band-aids, and got the house tidier before the grandparents arrived.

Sure, I expected questions about every bump and Band-aid. The grandparents did make comments like, "Boys are so rough and clumsy," and, "She must be having a growing spurt again." But through all the normal childhood bumps and even the day an ambulance was called, none of the grandparents ever suggested we neglected our kids. Of course not – my parents saw us twice a week, and my in-laws had raised three kids, including Bernie. They knew what active kids are like, and they knew what our home was like, from dropping by anytime.

I'll bet another reason they don't make nasty comments about the everyday bumps and bangs is because that would invite comments on the condition in which the kids come home after a day out with the Grandparents. It's not just the grass stains and skinned knees after feeding the ducks in the park - I'd never mention that. And the two-scoop ice cream cones eaten half an hour before dinner aren't really worth bringing up for discussion, especially while the kids are jazzed up and running around the house. No, that's not worth kicking up a fuss about, not when the kids are clutching new toys. We're talking birthday quality, not cheap pocket toys, for pity's sake. "It's Saturday. I wanted to give them a treat," says the doting grandmother.

One Saturday my daughter came home from buying milk at the supermarket with her Opa (paternal grandfather), clutching a one kilogram bag of jelly beans in both hands. "Lila said, 'Sometimes Mommy gives us these,'" reported the grandfather, gruffly. "It won't hurt her to share with her brother."

Well, it wouldn't hurt unless she dropped that huge bag on her foot. It took months for them to finish that bag of jelly beans. I doled them out, one at a time, with Band-aids, when the kids had "owies."

Starting a Writers' Workshop

When I began a weekly writers' workshop in "The Cove," an inner-city community association building in Victoria, my main goal was to get in touch with other beginning writers. We got in touch, all right: women and men, teenagers and the retired, university graduates and dyslexic illiterates. And we wrote, and we wrote, and we wrote.

There were poems, stories and personal essays. We held public readings and put on a writers' festival. Some of us wrote graffiti without guilt on sidewalk chalking days; others found words to write personal feelings. For all of us, there was the relief that here were other people who cared about writing, too, and whether their words said what they thought.

I knew from Creative Writing courses in University that feedback helped me to write better, and commenting on other people's writing helped me look more carefully at stories and poems. A workshop with my friends had been an incentive to keep writing after my twins were born, especially since one other member knew what it was like to type one-handed while cuddling a baby. At The Cove, I continued to learn by working with people from different backgrounds and with varying skills.

I learned that we could depend on our core of three members who came weekly for two years, bringing poems or stories almost every week. We were volunteers at The Cove and parents of toddlers, so this was our major social and "professional" contact of the week. We could also depend on four or five members to attend weekly for three to five months each. The workshop was continually changing around its common core as we got jobs, moved, or weathered crises.

There were always at least two participants who were mentally ill, including one of our three core members. We never had any disturbing incidents, only one argument. They were members like the rest: some brought poems weekly for four months, some wrote stories regularly, if not with complete literacy, and some attended a few times before moving on. One dropped in one evening on our monthly open-mike reading. With her head shaved and a glassy stare, she recited her poem beginning, "Who owns the rights to God?" The impact was stunning.

Moments like that could not be predicted, but the regular pattern of the workshop was consistent. We started at our regular time on Friday afternoons, with tea and coffee already brewed, and paper and pens ready for use. Sitting around a table, we listened as poems were read aloud. Stories were usually photocopied and taken home for members to read and scribble notes on, but were sometimes read aloud. We spent up to an hour giving our reactions and suggestions to two or three pieces of writing.

For a change of pace, we'd refill the coffee cups and one of us would read aloud an essay from Natalie Goldberg's *Writing Down the Bones*. This book has suggestions, exercises, anecdotes and encouragement. Reading it made most of us want to keep writing. It didn't matter whether we wrote the Great Canadian Novel or letters to our aunts. Some of us wanted to be professional authors and some wanted to write private feelings for our journals. Goldberg's essays encouraged us to write.

After reading an essay, or instead of it, I would pass around newspaper clippings from the Books Pages of the local papers or the Saturday edition of the Globe and Mail. Local news was mentioned, such as coffeehouse readings or the launch we held for a neighbour's local history book. Anyone who had heard of a writing contest or a magazine needing submissions would share the address and other information. Books and magazines were sometimes lent among members. We also kept in touch with the provincial writers' association and shared the newsletter.

After about twenty minutes, we'd get back to the serious business of workshopping each others' writing for up to another hour. We stopped on time, and members hung around afterward to chat, pick up the stories for next week and then catch the bus.

The time involved? Two hours, weekly. The expense? Those who had any money that week tossed 25 cents into the tea and coffee fund. The Cove gave us paper and a reasonable number of photocopies, and some members who could afford it had copies made of their own stories. The space needed? Enough room for everyone to sit around a table.

The most important thing we learned was how to make useful comments on each others' writing without being cruel. Even the dullest or most upsetting story deserves politeness, after all, and writers are often very sensitive to the difference between, "I couldn't see why your character did that," and, "It was a boring story." This doesn't mean we only said nice, bland things - we tried to show where the writing worked, where it didn't, and what we thought the writer could do to make it better.

One of our members used foul language almost every time she spoke, yet she never once called any of us a foul name. Another member was considerate when reading stories that didn't follow his personal moral standards. And we all learned to state our opinions so that they didn't bruise the people who would be reading our own stories and poems next week.

Aside from being considerate to one another, each writers' group makes its own workshop rules, such as asking the authors to wait until the end of the discussion to reply to comments. Usually everyone participates as writer and critic, but it soon becomes clear that even published writers may be lousy at analyzing a story or talking about it; and beginners may have been reading for fifty years and know what makes an interesting story tick. We encouraged each other to keep writing and to send our work to magazines and book publishers. After all, somebody writes those community papers and best-seller romance novels!

One member sent her "true confession" romance story about treeplanters to *Treeplanters Association* magazine. The editor bought it, though he'd never printed anything but factual articles and ads before. "It was about real treeplanters," the acceptance letter said. "It was about us. How could we not want to read it?" We at the workshop cheered her first professional sale.

There are five rules for professional writing, according to the late Robert Heinlein:

-You must write.

-You must finish what you write.

-You must send your writing to a publisher.

-If it is returned, keep sending your writing to new markets.

-Refrain from excessive re-writing unless to meet an editor's directions.

As beginning writers, whether or not we ever hoped to sell our work, we found that joining a writers' group helped each of us tremendously, as writers as well as in our home lives. Just being able to express myself better made me feel like a more competent person and a better parent, as I began writing stories that other people enjoyed reading. Working together, for a year or for just a month, gave feedback and a sense of community that went a long way.

My Christmas Wish List

A telephone that rings only if I really want to take that particular call from that person at that time and takes messages, silently, from everybody else except salespeople.

A BOX OF INTERLOCKING Lego or Meccano-style pieces that automatically picks up all the scattered bits when I press a button.

A TAPE RECORDER THAT will secretly record an acquaintance saying, "It must be nice to be a homemaker instead of working," and then send the tape to his own mother and wife.

A CHOCOLATE CHIP COOKIE recipe which tastes better than just any old stuff sticking chocolate chips together.

A STATE-OF-THE-ART computer system that keeps my records, does my taxes, prints my stories and letters and, at the press of a button, protects itself from juvenile damage when my kids type their homework and letters to Grandma.

BUBBLE BATH THAT SMELLS good without costing a lot or giving my kids rashes.

BUSINESS CARDS THAT read, "Don't tell me I'm a good parent – offer to BABYSIT."

Drink to Me Only With Thine Eyes
and Don't Spill!

Camping with kids is frustrating. Shopping with kids is frustrating. Shopping for camping supplies with kids in tow has been known to cause fallen arches and hair loss, and will lose the customer any sympathy a sales clerk may retain at four o'clock on a Friday in a stuffy store filled with $600 raincoats.

Our family goes for picnics, to outdoor festivals, or camping often in summer. We've been gradually adding to our camping supplies as our finances allow, and hope to buy the ultra-light, ultra-warm sleeping bags some day; maybe when we no longer have to worry about one of the kids throwing up in the tent. Ben has already made plans for the future.

"Hey, Mommy! Maybe I can get a real nice sleeping bag and a ten-speed bike, and then bike all the way across Canada! Maybe when I'm sixteen?" Maybe I'll just lock him up to protect him from bears and muggers. No, I have a better idea. I'll send his dad with him. Bernie hitch-hiked across Canada when he was eighteen. He'll like doing the trip in style, carting along all the camping gear, especially the propane campstove he likes to cook on. That's the one with the big, heavy propane tank and two burners so dinner gets cooked faster, with more pots to wash.

Some of our dishes and food containers are Tupperware or the like, but we get travel mugs when local businesses are having promotions and give-aways. These travel mugs usually have lids and are hard to spill or break, and cheap and easy to replace. All of these are important virtues for picnic supplies.

As handy as these plastic travel mugs are, the ad slogans printed on some of them are not my cup of tea. When a mug reads, "Levasole, the topical cattle worming system" - well, I find it hard to drink from. And if you turn it around, the other side isn't always any better: "Tetraject - a long acting broad spectrum antibiotic."

So we got Sierra cups for our family, which are deep enough for cups and, in a pinch, wide enough to serve as small bowls. Small servings mean lots of helpings, but also less gets spilled each time. It pays off, for one kid or another always spills during a picnic or camping trip... or during a snack break while shopping for camping supplies.

I paid for a two-door Taymor tent on sale in Capitol Iron one day and discovered later that it was the one-door model, instead. When my two-year-old kids and I brought it back with the receipt, the Camping Supplies clerk offered me a refund, or credit on the purchase of a more expensive tent.

When I insisted on the advertised two-door tent, he shrugged and asked, "Whadda ya want me to do, lady, cut another door in the tent with a razor blade?"

My little ones stared up at him, blue eyes wide. "Mommy," asked one, moments later as we headed for the manager's office, "What's a jerk?"

Three minutes with the Sales Manager (while the kids played airplane around our chairs) confirmed Capitol Iron's standard policy of re-ordering new stock to match what was advertised. In a week I had the right tent, at the advertised price, from the hands of the same clerk who mumbled, "Have a nice day."

I thought that was the end of the frustration until I tried sleeping in that dome tent with a husband who snores, a daughter who burrows and a son who travels over the rest of us in his sleep. I could have taken the refund, after all.

Is It What They Say – Or How They Say It?

Waiting for the bus after daycare one day, the kids and I had a little talk about how, when they grew up, they could be anything they wanted to be. "Don't know, mama," one twin said doubtfully, while the other shook a tousled head.

"Sure you can. You can do anything you want to do in your life. You can go anywhere you want. You can be anything you want to be," I said encouragingly.

Ben's three-year-old chin stuck out at a decisive angle. "Alright. I wanna be a scientist. And a dinosaur. And green."

ON THE MOMENTOUS OCCASION of Lila's first visit to the dentist at age three, she chattered like a bird, charming the receptionist, dentist and hygienist with her exploration of the office and the goodies box. Her teeth were cleaned and inspected by the hygienist, who reported a small cavity in one baby tooth.

"Have you noticed this hurting a little?" she asked Lila, who answered, "Well, I noticed it a little."

"For how long – maybe a couple of weeks?"

"Oh yes," Lila agreed, "I think it was a couple of weeks."

"Hah!" said the hygienist, turning to look at me over her shoulder. "And I bet Mommy never even knew about this. What a bright, articulate child you have, not like most three-year-olds," she added.

"Oh yeah? Ask her if her tooth is blue," I said.

Puzzled, the hygienist turned back. "Is your tooth blue, dear?"

"Oh yes, I think it's quite blue," answered Lila.

This reply set the hygienist back on her stool, thoroughly baffled. "So what does this mean?" she appealed to me.

"It means," I sighed, "that while she can talk as well as a six-year-old, she doesn't make any more sense than a three-year-old normally does." (Lila knew what it meant – it meant she was getting a balloon *and* a sticker from the nice lady with the puzzled smile and the goodies box.)

WHEN I WENT TO DAYCARE one afternoon, Ben (almost four) was ready to be picked up, and had something to show me. "This is my picture. That is just the world. This is me. And the reason I'm so tall is I'm standing on your shoulders. And THIS is my name."

RIDING THE NINE O'CLOCK bus to daycare one morning, I looked up to see a man whom I knew slightly getting on at a bus stop. "Hi, John," said the driver, and John nodded to him and to me. "Mama," said Ben, not quite as quietly as I might have hoped, "that man is very small."

"Yes, he is," I said matter-of-factly while Lila commented in great delight and friendliness, "He isn't any bigger than I am."

John said in equally friendly tones, "That's right, I'm not very big at all. Do you know why?" He had the attention of every kid on the bus, and all of their mothers. "It's because I never ate all my vegetables, and the good food my mother gave me. So when your mother gives you vegetables, you'll eat them, won't you?"

"I sure will," Ben promised. Every kid on the bus nodded, and John returned the delighted smiles of all the mothers.

MY SIX-YEAR-OLD FRIEND, Evan, had a cold one spring, and muttered to himself one day, looking at his mother's leather model snake on a shelf next to a Kleenex box: "Snake Kleenex – so every time you blow your nose, you scare yourself."

AFTER A BRUSH CUT, my seven-year-old son inspected his quarter inch of hair with approval and announced: "Now, if I could just tape back my ears, I'd have a never-ending face!"

"GABBY, SIT!" LILA SAID to her uncle's half-grown dog as it jumped on her. "Gabby, down!" as the dog knocked her down. "Gabby likes me!" she said as the dog licked her face.

BERNIE CALLED A FRIEND, whose young son Ian answered the phone with impeccable manners. "I'm not sure my dad's here," Ian replied to Bernie's request. "Please wait for a minute and I'll see if he can come to the phone." Clunk went the receiver. Footsteps receded. "Daaaad!" came an unholy screech, clearly audible over the phone."Dad! Daaaad! DAD!"

More footsteps; Ian was crossing to another doorway by the sound of the next shrieks. "Daaaad! DAD! Daa-aad!"

Bernie heard a woman's voice saying, "What's all this about?"

"Dad has a phone call."

"Oh," said Ian's mom, with remarkable calm."Maybe he's out here."

"Daaaad!" Ian screeched, as if he were being gored by wild animals. "Dad! DAAAAD!" When the woman finally came to the phone to ask Bernie to call back later, he was shaking with laughter.

AT TEN O'CLOCK ONE evening, nine-year-old Lila stumbled out of her room and met our disapproving stares. "My toes can bend all the way backward!" she reported, eyes wide.

"A nation is shocked," Bernie replied, turning her around and scooting her back to her room. "Go to sleep."

"But it hurts to bend my toes backward that far," she said.

"So don't bend them that far," I told her. "Go to sleep."

"I want to call the doctor and tell her my toes can curl all the way backward," Lila protested, hanging back at the door.

"I'm sure if we called the doctor at ten o'clock to tell her your toes can curl all the way backward, she, too, would tell you to go to sleep." Bernie stood over her in the doorway.

Lila brightened. "I'm going to see her tomorrow anyway about my bad cough. I can tell her then. Good night!"

She did tell the doctor, who listened carefully and said in all seriousness, "Isn't that wonderful! You're double-jointed, or very flexible. Maybe you'll be a gymnast." To me she added quietly, "I have a daughter about the same age. Most kids just say, 'I dunno' when I ask them how they feel. Isn't this great?"

BEN BROUGHT A NOTE out of his room when he was seven. "I made my plans for summer vacation," he said. The note read: "I want to spend a week in my rume with all my comik books, my komic cardz, the TV set, my toaster and the radio, and stay in bed all day with nootrishus snaks." The nootrishus snaks idea made it appealing enough that Bernie figured he deserved to try it for at least a day. Ben lasted the morning before staggering out, eyes bloodshot. "Man, do I have a lot of comics!"

Whatever Works

There are a thousand "best ways" to do everything, and a million "hints" to make life easier. What do I do to make things better? Whatever works.

The advice of my mother, my doctor, my mother-in-law, my friends, and the Parent Discussion Group, gave me a whole armada of tools to deal with my kids' coughs and colds. There was the steamer, cough syrup, liquid honey, and an electric heater a friend brought over in case the furnace ran out of oil. Garlic for spaghetti sauce if the twins were hungry. Warm drinks. Even two big chunks of amethyst crystal for putting under their pillows.

Did I use any of it? Hey, I used all of it. Nothing says you can't put a big crystal under the pillows of kids who just took their prescription medicine. I tried prayer. And a little positive visualization helped the kids imagine themselves getting better, something that's almost impossible on day two of the 'flu.

Lila had an awful cold when she was three, and began to wheeze. So we went to the doctor's office, where she instantly began to breathe more easily and stopped coughing. What is it about the air in the doctor's office that makes symptoms temporarily better? Someday someone is gonna bottle Doctor's Office Air and make a million bucks.

Luckily, she coughed again before we left, and the doctor heard her. Lila spent the night and the next day in hospital, where I learned what Bernie had been through with Ben and the pear-chunk in his bronchial tree a year earlier: as long as the kid is going to be okay soon, the hardest part is sleeping in an armchair or down the hall in the parents' room bunk beds.

The night in hospital was pretty tense, with Lila in an oxygen mask, but then the night before had been pretty tense, too, with her hacking and propped up on six pillows. She went home with a diagnosis of mild asthma and a bottle of the worst-tasting medicine. This medicine was supposed to be swallowed four times a day. We tried rewarding her with Popsicles, which were good for her sore throat, but the medicine was so yucky Bernie decided she could suck the Popsicle first, so it would numb her tongue. Even so, half the time she'd retch and bring the medicine right up. Who knew how much she really swallowed?

The second day, as she stormed at me and wouldn't open her mouth, I held her jaw open with my thumb and poured the vile spoonful down her throat. Lila gurgled and burst into tears. "Why did you do that?" she demanded.

"It's how you give dogs medicine," I said gruffly. "Dogs can't understand why they have to swallow yucky tastes."

"I'm not a dog!"

"No. But you were fighting like an animal that doesn't understand." An idea began to occur to me, combining creative visualization, prayer, and Lila's love for animals. We took the chalkboard and began to draw Lila Getting Better.

First she drew a doctor and a nurse, then herself in the big hospital bed. Then she drew her Medicine Helping Animal. "It's a dog, Mama," she said, "because I am good to dogs and they like me." The dog had its mouth held open with a thumb, "because dogs don't understand," she sighed. Next to it she drew the bottle of medicine. Every time after that, she held the spoon herself, looked at her chalkboard drawing, and downed her medicine.

We still went through a lot of Popsicle halves before she got a prescription for a nicer tasting medicine. She didn't need it more than twice a year or so, and she got a "puffer" at a much younger age than many kids with asthma. The doctor said she understood taking medicine pretty well. I think explaining it to her beat holding her down, no contest. Whatever works.

Music Hath Charms

There's an old saying: "Music hath charms to soothe the savage breast." But sometimes I think if I hear "Twinkle, Twinkle Little Star" one more time, I'm going to beat mine. My teeth grind at generic poppy tunes by glassy-eyed kids' show hosts who are peppier than I will ever be, even running from a wasp nest. "Kookaburra sits on eyectwic wiya," sings Ben with some entertainers from Down Under. "Tears in his eyes anniz pants on fiya. Ouch! Kookaburra, Ouch! Kookaburra, hot ya tail must be."

But just when I was ready to give up and let my two-year-olds play Bernie's old David Bowie albums, a few musical gems made music a family experience for us again.

When weather or the sniffles keep the kids indoors, and they've watched so much TV their eyeballs are flat on the front, it's cassette tapes that sometimes make a little peace at our place. Readings of the twins' favourite stories get played so often the tapes wear out, so it was with real relief that Bernie tried Valdy's *Kids' Album*. Unlike the run-of-the-mill Mother Goose rhymes or counting jingles, this tape has songs a folk-music fan would want to hear and might even learn to sing along.

The kids didn't always like the same music as they got older. One was still listening to Sharon, Lois and Bram but for her sixth birthday wanted Michael Jackson's *Black or White* tape. The other listened to his Dick Tracey tapes, avidly turning pages of the comic book and chanting the theme music. We learned that on their school bus, if everybody's good the driver turns on the local rock music station. If they're really good the volume goes up. I guess a back beat is easier on the driver than scuffles and goofing around in the back of the bus.

So, our sweet, angel-faced seven-year-old daughter learned all the words to "Only to be With You" and "Let's Talk About Sex." Who knows what she'll be listening to when she's a teenager?

There is a bit of a generation gap for musical preferences in our home. Bernie would rather play weird – er, experimental – music albums and sing along; my son improvises his own scat and bebop vocals for old folk songs – usually when his sister is singing an arrangement of "Jamaican Farewell" that's never been any further south than Motown.

I'm glad to see that there's music meant for families in the music stores as well as at music festivals. Sometimes all it takes is a single lyric, like the Travelling Willburys singing, "I've been robbed and ridiculed/ in daycare centres and night schools/ Handle me with care" to get parents in daycare centres and night schools across a continent singing bits of a song, all that season, while rocking their kids. It sure beats another chorus of "Twinkle, Twinkle Little Star."

It Was A Joke

Apparently a good comedian has to have good timing and good delivery. My son appears to be a born comedian even though he had a rough delivery, because he's certainly having a good time.

Ben has been a comedian all his life, starting with peek-a-boo and parades draped in crib blankets. April Fool's Day is as important as Hallowe'en on his calendar. But all this humour and joke-making isn't only following the lead of his father, the man who once put a Christmas light blinker on the power cord of my typewriter. But young Ben does not imitate his father's jokes. He makes up his own jokes.

Taking the twins to daycare one morning, we noticed our three-year-old son was giggling all the way to the bus stop. He lugged his suspiciously heavy lunch kit. It rattled in a funny way, too, but he wouldn't let us open it. Finally, as the bus was arriving, he admitted that he had put a potato inside.

"A potato?" It was a big one, too. Was he that hungry?

"I took it so that when it's lunch time, and everyone takes out their sandwiches, then I'll take out my potato," he explained. "And everybody will say, 'Ben! You have a potato in your lunch!' And they'll go gunnngg!" He mimed slack-jawed, goggle-eyed surprise.

"Good idea," said his father, closing the lunch box and waving for the bus. "Let us know how it works out."

Later, when we picked the twins up at daycare, we spoke to Lila first. "How did Ben's potato joke go?"

"Just like he wanted. Everybody went duh-hh!" she rolled her eyes. "I have a weird brother." We agreed and Bernie went to congratulate his son on the joke's success. It wasn't the first time. It wouldn't be the last.

Some months later, there was a sleepy Sunday morning when two newspapers and the teapot held more appeal for me than conversation. Ben crept under the edge of the section of the weekend paper I was reading and said: "Mom? When I was a little baby, curled up inside your tummy, I used to sleep on a stack of folded newspapers." His eyes lit up at my smile. "That was a joke," he added, climbing up for a hug.

There's a little rubber gecko lizard he moves around the house. It's been found on the fridge, the smoke detector (he had to stand on the back of the couch to put it there) and last night it was in my hair. That joke didn't work so well. Both kids learned new words when I discovered the little creature tickling my ear and flung it across the room. When my heart rate slowed down, Ben apologised and went off to brush his teeth for bed. Later, Bernie opened the bathroom door to find toilet paper streamers swaying from the doorknob around the toilet seat and back again. How did Ben rig it without breaking the paper when he closed the door? The first ones broke, so he set up longer pieces. Practice makes perfect.

Now Ben is older. He's lost the baby-cuteness, but never the light in his eyes when he takes the lint from the dryer, soaks it and puts it outside the door to his sister's room for Lila to step on and shriek.

I can't discourage this streak of humour in Ben, and wouldn't if I could. When I take his comic books away at bed time, he lies giggling in the dark.

A Conversation Between Friends

When my friend Ruth (not her real name) and I get together for an evening, we usually end up at her house or mine, drinking coffee and talking till ten o'clock. One night it was her ex-husband's turn to baby-sit, so she came over to my house.

She phoned ahead, so the kettle was already on when she knocked and let herself in, saying: "Hi, it's me. How're my godchildren doing?"

"They're asleep already, and Lila's cold is better." I put two Earl Grey teabags into the teapot. "So, how's my goddaughter doing?"

"Still awake when I left, but Daddy's on kid patrol tonight." Ruth pulled one of the kitchen chairs out from the table, sat and slouched. "I am sooo tired. It's been..." She waved her hands dramatically.

"One of those days?" I put out two mugs and the sugar.

"One of those weeks," she sighed. "Between Daycare and Social Services, it's been hairy."

Taking another chair at the table, I nodded. "What's been hairy this time?" I poured tea for both of us.

Ruth sighed. "Well, you remember about eight weeks ago when my little one started rubbing her bottom, as she called it, once in awhile before falling asleep?" She put two spoons of sugar into her mug, stirred and handed me the spoon.

"Yeah, we talked about it then, and decided she must have figured out how to masturbate all on her own, by accident. The books said some kids do. Oh, and she didn't do it that night she stayed here, last week."

"You told me then." Ruth sipped her tea. "She does it once or twice a week, and wouldn't have done it here because I told her Friday that rubbing her bottom is a private thing, and not for at Auntie's house or Daycare."

I began to see what might have been Ruth's hassle this week. "Did she do it at Daycare?" My hands circled my mug.

Ruth nodded. "Friday naptime, and the Daycare worker just told her it was time to sleep. The worker mentioned it to me that afternoon, and I told her about the books and pamphlets you and I were reading. It was no problem."

"But?" My tea was growing cooler; I drank deeply now.

"Monday, she decided to get one of the books for herself from Social Services, and they asked her point blank if any kids in her Daycare were masturbating." Ruth looked down. "When she said yes, they told her she had to report it to the Child Abuse Hotline, because masturbation is one of the signs of sexual abuse." Her face flamed with embarrassment and outrage.

"Oh, no! What did she do?"

"She refused to give any names," Ruth told me. "She told the social worker that she knew the signs of abuse and didn't think that this was the case. And she wanted the book anyway, because she wanted to know more about masturbation. She said she doesn't do it, but that doesn't mean it's not normal."

I poured more tea for Ruth. "And was that it?"

"No," Ruth admitted miserably. "The book came to the Daycare in the mail, of course. And today a phone call came from the social worker. She just wanted my Daycare worker to know that she'd put in a report to the Child Abuse Hotline, herself, saying that one of the children at the Daycare was probably being sexually abused."

My heart sank. "But your daughter's not being abused!"

"You know that. I know that. My ex-husband knows that. My parents know that." Ruth ticked her points off on her fingers. "And, thank God, my Daycare worker knows that."

The kitchen seemed awfully quiet. "So, what did she do when she got this call?"

Ruth smiled, showing a row of white, sharp teeth. "She hit the roof. She told the social worker that she had made it clear she knew the signs of abuse and didn't think this un-named child was being abused in any way. She reminded the social worker that she, too, was a trained professional and her judgment in this area was completely dependable."

She relaxed a little in her chair. "And just for good measure, she told the social worker that of the twenty children in her care as a Daycare Supervisor, two were being counselled as subjects of child abuse. There were no parallels with this case, and she refused to identify the child."

"She trusted you," I said with relief.

Ruth nodded. "She trusted her own judgment, too. If she had the faintest idea any child was being abused, she'd be the first to report it. But even with someone from Social Services pressuring her, she believed her own judgment and she believed me."

"Oh, Ruth." Thinking about it made me dizzy. "You could have had your kid taken away without any trial or anything. She wouldn't have been there when you came to pick her up this afternoon."

"I guess it's gotta be that way, for kids who are being hurt and all, and the trials come after," Ruth said slowly. "But I never thought it could be used against me. I never abused my kid, or taught her to jack off. I've never masturbated in my life, I wouldn't want to."

I blinked. "Oh, well, I don't know how people would get by, if no one ever did that."

Ruth stared at me for a minute, then laughed. "So maybe my daughter's not going to grow up to be a maniac, or grow fangs and fur all over."

We laughed together. "Well, what did the books say?" I wiped my eyes. "If my three-year-old goddaughter decides to rub her bottom once a week before falling asleep, I'm not going to worry. Are you?"

"Nope," Ruth answered. "And if either of my godchildren jacks off as a teenager, are you going to worry?"

"Nope. But I'll probably read more about it then and try to talk with them. Or get their dad to." I topped up our mugs with the last of the tea. "Thanks for talking with me about this."

Ruth shook her head. "No, thank you for letting me babble on about what's on my mind. And for being there two months ago when I was looking for books and someone to talk with about it. You really helped."

"Unh-unh. We helped each other. And that's the truth."

Small Business Has Been Good To Me

Oh, there are national corporations, and franchises across the country, but give me a small, locally-owned and -operated business every time.

"John's Place" Bakery was the place we wandered into on a family togetherness outing. (All right, it was a "date" with my husband, and the kids were along too.) The owner came out to serve us cookies himself, poured Bernie a cup of coffee from the employees' coffee maker, and went back into the kitchen to find two glasses of milk for the twins. "It's our first day. We've been open an hour. How do you like us so far?" asked the owner. "I've gotta put some tables and chairs up front, and a cooler and coffee maker behind the counter. People are gonna want to eat in like you, not just take out." Does this sort of thing happen at the Bread Factory a few blocks away? Nope. Trucks pull in and out of there, not families.

I'd rather give my money to a local business, instead of the local branch of a big company. When we rented the house, the "Multi National Oil" representative said that since we had to buy the quarter-tank of furnace oil anyway, why not pay for a service contract?

"Let me get this straight," I said to the service representative. "You want me to give you money now, so that in a year, I can pay again to have the furnace inspected, and if it needs repair, I can pay again for parts and labour? So what exactly am I buying now?"

"The guarantee that you'll get service when you need it," he chirped.

I never bought furnace oil from them again. There was a small company around the corner that always delivered oil the day I phoned. Oldfield Oil didn't insist on a quarter-tank minimum, either. Lots of their customers bought fifty or a hundred dollars' worth at a time, rather than pony up two or three hundred dollars all at once. People on a low income notice things like that. Oldfield Oil had a lot of loyal customers.

So, when the furnace died one February (of course it was during a cold snap) I called Oldfield. They didn't do repairs, but they knew a small business man who did... He came out that evening after supper, because there were kids in the house. He told my property manager to buy a new burner, and he installed it that evening, because he was a dad, and he didn't want to imagine little kids being cold.

While all this was going on, Ben and Lila were having friends in for a birthday party sleep-over. What a circus! When the kids went to sleep, the sounds of furnace repair kept on filtering steadily up from the basement.

I began baking so the oven would keep the kitchen warm. Cookies for the jar, biscuits for breakfast, and I baked a pie for the repair man who went beyond the call of duty and got the new furnace burner working before 11:00 pm. He also drank coffee and ate a plate of cookies.

Compare that to repair technicians from big businesses who say they'll come on Monday but don't, and then don't even phone till Tuesday. Give me a small business every time. Small business has been good to me.

Welcome to Parent Hell

There are the worst days, and there are the worst days. Calling Poison Control to find out if Zincofax ointment is poisonous when eaten, only to be told by a doctor, "Oh, hell, I don't know for sure. Get the kids to Emergency and we'll give 'em syrup of ipecac." Coming down with the flu the same time as the twins and Bernie, so that we all lay around for days, croaking and drinking juice, feeling like death on a soda cracker. Having a car accident with the twins and two neighbour kids in the car, and being told by someone, "It looks like gas is leaking out of the back of your car!"

"Out! Everybody out of the car right now!" It wasn't gasoline, it was a broken jug of water, but still.

Picnics, every one of 'em. Compared with the big one. And even as it happened, I knew that worse happens, and I don't know how parents live through the worst.

Our worst day was when Ben's feet were crushed under a boulder.

Printed words do not show how slowly my hands moved to write that. It sounds so melodramatic. Here I spent five years worrying about traffic, corrosive cleansers and vaccinations against life-threatening illness... and a boulder that hadn't been there an hour earlier appeared in the neighbour's yard.

Pause to drink deeply from mug of tea. Rub trembling hands. Pull it together because this is the big one.

Everybody's kid gets hurt or sick some time, a little or a lot, and the parents go through agonies of guilt, wishing they could make it not happen. This is the hardest thing to talk about, or write about, but I'm doing that here because it helps better than anything else to put to rest the voice of guilt and hurt. There is no right answer, no one word to make everything better. But shutting up will not help.

I am not writing about this to make our family seem heroic or victimized. Everyone has their own worst day, and if we're lucky we get through it with someone to talk with and hold.

We were planning to go away for a few days, and spent the morning packing knapsacks and cleaning house. When we wanted lunch, I ran across the street to the gas station and corner store, noticing that the neighbour's house had a truck in the driveway again. After lunch, the kids told Bernie they wanted to go next door to tell the boy who lived there that we'd be away for a few days. We heard the kids run next door, me washing dishes and Bernie in the bathroom. The next thing we heard was Lila calling for help.

Bernie called to me. I was out the door and over the fence before I actually heard what Lila was saying: "Come quick, Ben has a rock on his feet!" She was standing in the neighbours' backyard, calling in through their window. Behind her, on the driveway, was a heap of boulders as high as my head. Beside the heap was a very large stone. And Ben was on his hands and knees, with his feet trapped under the boulder.

At least a dozen things went through my mind at once. How the hell did those boulders get there? Ben is moving his head and crying. His feet must be gone. We'll get him prosthetics. He may need tourniquets – and for the first time in days, I'm not wearing a kerchief headband. I'll *kill* that landlord, I swear I'll tear out his liver and make him eat it. *He put boulders in the yard of a house he rented to a woman with a little kid.* Thank God it isn't *her* kid, she'd be having hysterics instead of getting help. Ben needs help. Lila called for help – oh no, she saw it happen.

It took only a second, and things slowed down enough that I could talk. "Okay, sweetie, I'm here now. Good for you." My mouth was dry. I patted her and went past to Ben. Everything had sharp edges, all the sounds seemed unusually clear, and I could hear Ben's breath whistling in as he screamed in terror.

He calmed when I touched him and spoke to him, but when I put my hands on the rock it wouldn't move. That was the only moment I felt ready to shriek and panic myself. Shouting for help scared Ben again, and when Bernie arrived an ageless five seconds later, I was kneeling with Ben across my lap. "Okay, Ben, Daddy's here, too," he said. "Lila, go get the first aid kit from my knapsack." She ran.

"You can move your head and arms all you want," I told Ben. "And you can cry all you like. But you mustn't move your legs. And you don't need to scream, Daddy and I are right here." But we couldn't move the boulder.

The neighbour, Stephanie, came out, with her boyfriend, Ray, and a visitor. All three men got a good grip on the boulder, knees bent, ready to lift. They were cranked on adrenaline, their veins standing out, muscles straining. It could have been bedrock. It didn't even quiver. "Stop," I said desperately. "You're hurting yourselves. You'll all bust a gut and it isn't moving." They tried again, faces red and teeth clenched.

Stephanie gulped air behind me, and I turned to tell her: "Call 911. Tell them the address. Say compound fracture. Get here right away." She nodded, freckles standing out on pale skin, and ran. The men fell back, breathing. Bernie came round the boulder, looking for some way to use the first aid kit Lila brought. There was no way to get at Ben's feet, trapped between the rock and the driveway made of sharp, newly broken gravel pounded into place.

Then Bernie saw Ben's left foot. He screamed. Quietly. He still had no breath. I never want to hear such a sound again. It tore at me even more than Ben's screams for help. This was horror. Up till then he had only seen Ben's right foot, trapped in its sneaker, half under the boulder. This joint was crushed with bone and marrow exposed. We tried to dig gravel out from under his foot, but the gravel was hard-packed and wouldn't come up. It tore our hands and knees.

Ray disappeared somewhere as a police officer came up. He put the end of his nightstick under the boulder near Ben's left foot, and tried to lever up the boulder. His nightstick bent in a half-circle. "That won't work," I said. "We need a dead lift. We had four of us lifting, and couldn't budge it."

"We'll get something," he said desperately. Bernie picked up Lila as an ambulance and fire engine pulled up at the curb. One of the paramedics was bringing out The Jaws of Life, a power tool that opens crushed cars, when up the driveway came exactly what we needed. I still see it in memory and it ends my nightmares.

It was a forklift. Ray had run to the brickyard a block away. The driver wore a very unhappy expression. He knew he'd have to do this right the first time. Carefully he lined up the forklift. Bernie carried Lila out of the way. Luckily Ben had seen forklifts many times before, probably even this one, on our walks around the neighbourhood. He wasn't afraid of its noise, even so close to him. The boulder came up at last.

I was still holding Ben, right next to the wheel of the forklift. I looked under the rock. Ben still had feet. The relief hit me so hard, it took the cop telling me three times, "Pull her out!" for me to understand that he meant Ben with his long hair. I gently pulled him out. When I stood up, lifting him, a firefighter came forward to take him.

"He's five years old, has no allergies and he weighs forty pounds," I said, hoping they'd give him something for pain. They laid him on the grass and cut away his high-top sneakers.

The sympathy on their faces, both police and paramedics, was clear when Ben wiggled his toes on request, then sat up, looked at his bruised and bleeding feet and screeched, "Oh no, I really hurt myself this time!" They told him he was a good boy, a wonderful kid, and they wrapped him up carefully and put him in the ambulance. They let me come, too.

The sympathy the police and paramedics were showing was not shared by a cameraman from the local television station. As Bernie was carrying Lila out of the way of the forklift, the cameraman was getting into the way. Most of the video he took was of Bernie's shoulder, which Bernie kept putting in front of the lens. Most of the sound he recorded wasn't used; "Get lost, you creep," was about the mildest thing Bernie said to him. The first that most of our friends heard of the injury was on the news.

The TV and newspaper reporters got Ben's full name from the accident report, so all the reports carried his name as Frank. People who knew we used Ben's middle name wondered whether or not this was our boy until they read the newspaper's quote from Bernie: "Welcome to parent hell."

"Once we read that," our friends said, "We knew it was you." And they usually added, "Can we help you tonight?" or, "I'm free tomorrow, do you need a ride anywhere?" Parent hell was less scary with all the phone calls, the homemade cards, and most of all, the talking over a cup of coffee or a mug of tea.

Guardian Angel

Ben's accident showed me how busy guardian angels are, and how many people acted as guardian angels for us. The police, who could have interrogated Bernie or me about how the injury occurred, instead summed up the situation in moments, realizing that no one expects an attractive nuisance like boulders to appear without warning or protection. The constable who bent his nightstick and gave Bernie and Lila a ride to hospital even dropped in on Ben a few days later, to give him a baseball cap and a handshake.

I've heard how some police and firefighters feel like they're protecting their city, like everyone in it is their kid, their brother or mother. It looked like that on our neighbour's lawn, with paramedics gently wrapping Ben's feet in half-casts, and one giving him oxygen. He didn't need oxygen, but it couldn't hurt, and it was what this firefighter could give him.

The ambulance driver called his wife, a nurse, to tell her that Ben would be coming into Surgery later. He told her what a terrific kid Ben was, and she had Popsicles and Fudgicles ready for when he came out of Surgery around midnight. He wanted them, too. Since he'd just had lunch before the accident, Ben had to wait until late that evening before he could have surgery.

If the minutes before the boulder was lifted were hell, waiting for surgery took an eternity. Ben was quickly hooked up to an IV. "Yeah, I have big muscles and veins, I'm very strong!" His injuries were checked by a doctor who at last gave him an injection for pain (after I'd babbled his age and weight at least three times). Bernie and Lila came in to sit with him for a while and he went for X-rays. The rest of the time Ben lay drowsy and in some pain.

He kept waking up in tears, needing to be reassured. "I felt like the boulder was taking me down to the centre of the earth," he told his dad. Bernie told him he could take a hammer and wear goggles and smash at that boulder. (The next day, when the boulder was broken into pieces for a rock wall, we brought him a piece and he whaled away on that with great satisfaction.)

The nurses brought Ben glycerine suckers and let us undress him. That was when we found the bruise and scrape as big as my hand on the small of his back. Ben's guardian angel had certainly been busy, keeping that rock off his back! And there were still six more hours to wait while Ben slept fitfully and moaned.

When Ben finally went into Surgery at eleven pm, I stumbled downstairs to phone Bernie, then wandered off to look for food. The Cafeteria was closed, but by the vending machines some people were drinking coffee and talking.

One of them looked at me. "You look pretty upset. Are you okay?" She looked kind of pale, herself.

"Yeah." I tried to smile for her. Wrestling with coins, I bought a chocolate bar and some chips. "I am pretty upset – my kid had his feet crushed under a boulder."

"Is he gonna be all right?"

I nodded. "They may pin his ankle."

"How old is he?" she asked.

"Five."

"My son is fifteen," she said, distantly. "He was in a car accident today. His chest was crushed."

"Is he gonna be all right?"

"They don't know yet," she said bleakly. There wasn't anything else to say. We ate and drank, standing together for a few minutes till one of her people spoke to her and she came there to answer. I walked a little away, to let them talk with the only thing I could give them – privacy.

That was all some people could give us, and it was usually enough. Wrestling a wheelchair around for a month was about as hard as pushing a stroller had been. Some people stared, but that might have been at Ben's bright cast covers with day-glo dinosaurs. People whose kids use chairs all the time must have the patience of saints. I ended up carrying Ben almost everywhere until he was allowed to crawl, and for most of another month.

Stephanie, the neighbour, brought over a get-well card. "I didn't fall apart!" she crowed. "I called 911 and even remembered my address. Last time my kid fell off the bunk bed and needed stitches, I cried so hard they had to give me a sleeping pill. This time I held it together!" When Ray came over, my dad (the blue-collar suburbanite) shook hands with him (the out-of-work drummer), thanking him for remembering the forklift was nearby.

When we wheeled into the brickyard, the office worker came out with a big smile. "I know who you are," she said, and went to get the forklift driver. He came over, younger than I'd thought, touching Ben's casts in awe. "Look at you! Oh, man!"

We encouraged Ben to think of himself as strong and getting better. We took photos and drew pictures of him and Lila, wearing costumes and fierce expressions, "being powerful." One of his toys in hospital was a rubber glove, blown up with a monster face inked on it. Ben loved his monster, and bounced it all over, with a spoonful of water rattling around inside. Out on the Cafeteria sundeck, it popped, spraying a lady to whom Ben made sincere apologies between gales of laughter. "What a great joke!"

Our families were very supportive, and at the end of that summer when Ben and Lila were both tall and strong and tan, one set of their godparents were proud to be there when we gave each twin souvenirs of their strength.

Ben took the shock of this whole event better than anyone could expect. He was terrific. So was Lila. Both kids cried and were stunned, but they talked and there was very little of the screaming that messes up parents' heads so nobody can think. What held them so calm, I'm not sure. Maybe it was that we expected the best out of our angels (the children or the guardians). We sure got it that day. We were a team.

Forgotten Territory

As soon as Ben's casts came off, we were on the road. Most of our belongings went into a storage locker. We had decided to live in a small farmhouse on land owned by Bernie's parents. We could learn market gardening, and keep our expenses down for a few years while Bernie completed his training in fine furniture making. The only problem was that the farm was north of Edmonton, about eight hundred miles from Victoria.

A journey of this scale in Europe could take us from Paris to East Berlin. Here in Canada, the money and language were the same, but there were cultural differences between the West Coast and Alberta. We felt as much like immigrants as the members of the East Indian family that were our nearest neighbours, a mile away.

The neighbours and people in the nearest towns were confused just looking at us. Bernie was the only man north of Edmonton with both an earring and a ponytail... *and* a female spouse. I was the only woman over twenty with long hair, and the only one over thirty who didn't style it with a perm. Keeping my maiden name confirmed it: we were hippies!

It took Bernie's parents a while to get over it. Meanwhile we helped Bernie's brother and sister-in law with their large market garden on one side of the farm, and learned to work our smaller garden. The quarter section of land (a square which is a quarter-mile on a side) had a big patch of bush and a large hayfield, perfect for the kids to ramble around on their own, so long as they stayed away from the well and the dugout pond.

Both twins helped pick vegetables. Ben crawled in the soft, dry dirt, picking potatoes. Before long he was dragging bucketsful along as he walked, his scarred ankle sinking into the freshly dug ground. Lila made friends with a piglet which her aunt had "liberated" from the SPCA where she worked. She would play and dance with the piglet, or on her own out in the hayfield, making up songs and dances.

In some ways, living on the farm was like stepping back into 1920; a forgotten territory where people weren't expected to live any more. I got a lot of questions about how hard it must be to live there, but honestly, I think Bernie had it harder than me. I caught him, at least once, leaning over the kettle on the gas stove with a mug in one hand and a spoon in the other, shrieking: "Instant Coffee! It's supposed to be Instant Coffee!"

And I only had to thaw out the pipes on my own once. The other times, he thawed them out. He re-plumbed and re-wired the little white farmhouse we lived in, and renovated the basement so Ben and Lila each had their own rooms. The 500 square feet of that tiny house held the four of us for three and a half years, and will again for a few summers to come. At least we had running water after the first summer.

As for the first winter, it was the coldest. We woke up one morning to CBC Radio saying that the coldest spot in Canada was about five miles north of where we lay shivering in bed. -54°C. I gave Bernie the look that all husbands dread and snarled, "I blame you for this." After he bundled up, went out and started my car so I could go to work as a Recreation Programmer in the next town, he put a space heater inside it and came back inside to kneel at my feet, saying "I'm sorry. I'm sorry. I'm sorry." He took the edge off his abasement by adding with a grin, "We'll be outside playing with the kids this afternoon, though. You can hear every sound for miles, even the lions roaring at the Wildlife Park." We did go out after I came home from work, of course. Ever try to stay indoors all day with two five-year-olds?

Moving to the farm meant almost no door-to-door salespeople dropped by, but those who did were so persistent I could only shake them off by offering to write advertising copy and sales pitches for them. Zoom! Gone like a shot. On the negative side, our long-distance phone bills tripled. We were really vulnerable to the TV ads that came out then, where families reunite because of special phone calls.

"I wanna call my Mom!" Bernie announced after one such ad.

"She lives next door, for crying out loud!" I giggled into the book I was reading at the kitchen table. "Go walk the half-mile to her place if not seeing her since lunch is too long!"

Even though there was a half-mile between the two houses on the farm, in many ways we were all living together and had to get along. I found the splendid isolation of walking alone in the backfield to be relaxing, with or without the kids along to Explore Wild Nature. And I became aware of the strangest thing: living in Victoria, there had been at least thirty people living within a block of our house, yet I could go days without seeing any one of them come and go, and sometimes not even hear the tenant in the upstairs duplex (the one who put on her hob-nailed boots to tap-dance her way to the bathroom at midnight). But from the little white house on the farm, we could see the lights of neighbour's houses two miles away, and know if they were home for the evening. Bernie would be out for a walk under the full moon, listening to owls and to trucks change gears two miles down the township road.

When we talked to friends and acquaintances in Edmonton or Victoria, it seemed that it had been generally forgotten that people ever lived where and how we did – in fact, that people still did live "way out there" was news to many. The people who lived on the acreages and in the small towns were similarly amused at our braids and tie-dyed t-shirts. "It's like you're living in one of those communes from the 1960's," said one neighbour. I didn't take offence; I was too busy with the collective farm work and shared minding of the twins and their cousins.

We have some place in that community now, though. Lila is friends with the neighbour girl, and Ben with every frog in the dugout pond. Bernie and I sell vegetables at the farmers' markets. One summer, one local man said to another at market: "Hey, it's your turn now to buy some veggies from that girl with the braid, let her tell you about using no sprays. Best carrots I ever tasted."

Sometimes I may feel as forgotten as the lions and tiger roaring a mile away in the Wildlife Park. But mostly I am getting a sense of territory here, of how big the wide open spaces really are and how much of it I can walk over and touch in any one day.

Kharma Repair Kit: Travelling with Kids

In Barriere, BC, we found the library, a bakery and an auto mechanic all open for business at nine a.m. This was welcome news for our family expedition: we had two kids, a U-Haul trailer with no signal lights, and a car with trouble. The stop could have been a miserable one, but we made it a chance for Kharma Repair.

Richard Brautigan wrote a poem entitled, "Karma Repair Kit: Items 1 to 4." The poem reads, in its entirety:

1. Get enough food to eat, and eat it.
2. Find somewhere to sleep, and sleep there.
3. Find the silence inside yourself, and listen to it.
4.

This constituted enough of a plan to make travelling with our five-year-olds in an eighteen-year-old Dodge Dart called Underfoot not only survivable, but something we repeated, for a total of three trips between Victoria, BC and Edmonton, AB that year.

Travelling is never comfortable when the kids (or adults, come to think of it) are hungry or tired. So we made food and rest stops regularly. We found family-run restaurants, or bakeries, or coffeeshops in every town, and they were a lot more relaxing and fun than the franchise restaurants' attitude of "feed 'em fast and clear 'em out for the next batch of customers." The twins loved spinning on the round seats at counters, the coffee was good and there was room for Bernie to spread out the morning newspaper. (Kharma repair for Bernie involves reading at least one newspaper a day.)

We also kept food and campstoves in the trunk so that dinner could be ready twenty minutes after pulling into a rest stop, cramped from sitting still in the car. The kids and one parent would come pounding back from "Exploring Wild Nature" as Ben put it, piggy-backed over rough ground and mountain streams, and they'd find barley and garlic, sardines, carrot sticks and peanut butter sandwiches ready for lunch. On the road we ate carrots, raisins, fruit leather, buns, and apples – packed before we left or picked up in stores along the way. My purse and pockets bulged with crinkling packets of snacks.

Why the emphasis on food? Because I'd found that most of the time when the kids got fussy and I lost my cool, somebody or other was just plain hungry. My kharma repair kit involved snacking on carrots so nobody would pester me for chocolate bars at the next gas station.

The regular food and rest stops gave Bernie and me a break from driving or being on "kid patrol." We found that, instead of having a numb bum from driving, we actually had energy to climb around parks having fun with the kids, and to enjoy driving through spectacular mountains and forests instead of yelling at whichever twin was kicking the back of the driver's seat. Starting out early meant we were able to travel a fair distance each day, even with all the pauses to watch waterfalls, elk beside the road, and bears fishing in river flats.

Sleep was easy to forget about till all of a sudden we'd need some. The kids could nap in the car, but at night we all wanted to lie down. If the urge hit us while the sky was still light, we set up our tent and were in bed in half an hour. Sleeping outdoors is an adventure that repairs my kharma. Thank heaven for dome tents! Room for all of us, even if my husband snores and my daughter rolls over and over. Even so, we chose motel rooms some nights when it was ten-thirty and raining. A comfortable sleep, whether in a motel bed or a sleeping bag in bear country, made the whole trip feel like a holiday.

A motel meant the kids watched half an hour of TV cartoons in the morning. A rest stop meant one parent read the paper while the other introduced the twins to squirrels and birds. A scenic view gave us time to focus on infinity, meditating peacefully, and walking around between lunch and a trip to the restroom. We made time for each other to rest and play or the trips would have been an exercise in misery, instead of travel.

There was an astonishing amount of just plain nothing on our trips, too. Nothing between Calgary and Edmonton, but fields and blue sky. Nothing that had to get done on time, so we spent two hours fishing in a small river. Nothing under the road for a very long way down into the Fraser Canyon. We didn't really have to do anything on these trips except get where we were going, together, before the money and fruit leather ran out.

The trips even ended up being kharma repair for Ben, whose feet healed that summer. It seemed like every gas station had a boulder or two for landscaping, and every rockslide had several. Ben was forever asking if this particular rock was okay to climb on, and comparing it to the size of the one that broke his feet. He was "King of the Castle" so many times that it became clear: Ben was on top of things like boulders now, thank you very much.

By the time we got to Barriere, we were cramped from driving, hungry and worried about our car and its signal light. Two hours later, we pulled back onto the Yellowhead Highway with everything in order. The twins had each had three books read to them at the library, met local dogs and cats and picked up souvenir rocks on a stroll around town.

The repairs were cheaper than we'd thought, and the mechanic had put us at the head of his priority list. After coffee and fruit juice at the bakery, we were on the road again, with a bag of fresh buns for later.

I mentioned the stop to my father, weeks later. "Barriere," he said. "Nice place to stop for a while."

It is.

Hospitality or Else

Living with Bernie's family in Alberta, and visiting his relatives was never boring; there were always either interesting people to talk with, or interesting things happening. Like the time Ben rolled down the basement stairs at Bernie's cousin's house. People didn't always react to these interesting things in the same ways, but that was part of what made it interesting.

Visiting Bernie's grandmother for a week was a holiday to remember. Stonewall, Manitoba, is full of the scent of blooming lilac trees in June. The kids loved going for walks along the small "downtown" area, where most of the buildings were a beautiful, cream-coloured limestone. Bernie's grandmother walked the kids and me down to the post office every day, and the kids usually managed to talk her into stopping at a candy store on the way back. They knew their "Knitting Grandma" was a pushover.

She was called "Knitting Grandma" because of all the mittens, touques, and sweaters she made. Each of her sixteen sons and daughters has a hand-knitted bedspread, and so do most of the grandchildren and great-grandchildren. Two of the littler ones have received Christmas packages with enough mittens to give every kid in their classrooms a pair. "Well, what am I going to do, just sit around?" Knitting Grandma snorted in explanation.

I don't know how she does it. I can't always find time to floss my teeth, let alone knit mittens for sixty kids each fall. Even knitting whenever she sat down didn't make her look rushed. She made me feel so welcome that I slept in till seven o'clock the first morning; and when I got up, I could hear the kids' voices in the kitchen, having breakfast.

Breakfast was big bowls of Rice Krispies and ice cream. Hunh?

"Knitting Grandma's freezer had a power failure," said Ben.

"Yeah! and all her ice cream's melting, so we gotta eat it!" Lila chimed in. Their eyes were already whirling with pent-up energy.

"Let them have a treat. It's a holiday," said their Knitting Grandma. A little later she commented, "They certainly are very energetic kids, aren't they?" as the twins ran around and around the rooms of her small house. I took them for a long, long walk around the limestone quarry. Next morning, they got up earlier so they could have ice cream for breakfast again. We went for a lot of walks that holiday.

The best way to visit Bernie's family and relatives is to smile and nod, nod and smile through the introductions, meals, barbecues, football games or whatever is going on. The hospitality for visitors, especially people one will probably never see again, is particularly warm. When my sister-in-law's brother, Ralph (that's my husband's brother's wife's brother, if anyone is keeping track) stopped by Bernie's parents' house one afternoon, there was a family gathering already in progress. He made the mistake of saying, "I can't stay long, my fiancée is waiting in the car."

"Well, bring her in to meet the rest of us," he was told.

"No, no, no, we have to drive down to High River, we can't stay," he protested. My mother-in-law repeated the direction, but he refused gently. "She's a little shy of meeting so many people."

"Well, if she won't come in to meet us, we'll all go out to meet her," announced my mother-in-law. With the twins holding onto their Oma's hands, she led a parade of both her sons and daughter, their spouses, her sister with spouse and two daughters, and my father-in-law, who brought up the rear after closing the front door behind the parade.

While lined up along the sidewalk, waiting our turn to lean into Ralph's sports car and shake hands with Ralph's fiancée, my brother-in-law turned to me and said sourly, "You've heard of Toys R Us? Well, this is Hospitality Or Else." He said it quietly, though, as he was next in line to be introduced by our mother-in-law to the young woman who smiled through clenched teeth. Smile and nod. Nod and smile.

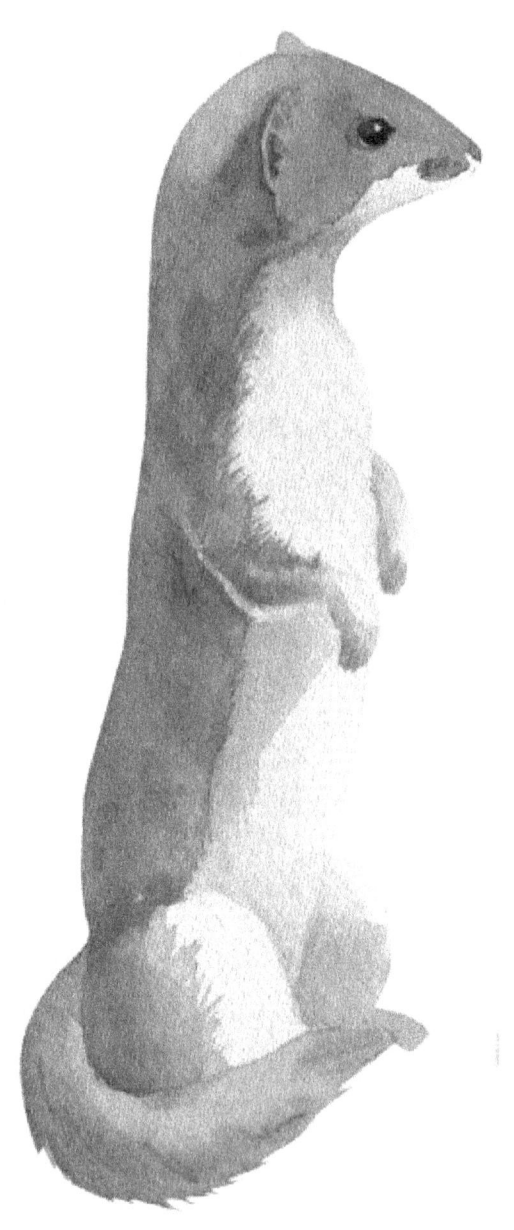

Trying Times

I'm trying to write Science Fiction stories and novels these days. Sometimes I'm trying my family's patience as well, but some writing does get done, as well as some of my household chores. On good days.

On a good morning, we all wake up on time, eat hot oatmeal while reading *The Globe and Mail*, get the kids out to the schoolbus and have all the farm chores done before 8:00 am. On a not-so-good morning, the kids ask me to buy the new cereal with 3-D hologram sparkles, and scribble with their colour-changing markers till the bus goes by and I drive the twins ten miles to the community school.

When things are going well at my word processor, I write short stories or a chapter from the novel in progress. When the power is disconnected by my husband during renovations on this old farmhouse, I scribble letters on note paper to my grandparents, asking them about their cardiograms and corneal transplants.

Sometimes I take a break and heat up lunch in the microwave, or just nibble on organic cookies with Brazil nuts from the Rain Forest. Sometimes, in the middle of the day, we drive fifty miles to Edmonton to FAX something I've written, especially during a postal strike.

I lose writing time if the answering machine isn't taking my calls. There may be few door-to-door salesmen out here; however, as compensation, automatic dialling systems leave messages about steam-cleaners for Dacron II rugs or a deluxe car wash which hand-cleans black cars only.

Even with all the distractions, I will occasionally stop writing Science Fiction and put a little effort into saving this world, one environmentally-conscious letter at a time. One week I decided to write to Parliament about the plight of a Russian cosmonaut still in orbit three months after he was due to return to Earth. Since the Soviet Union had disintegrated, there were no funds to pay his ground crew the price of a Canadian movie ticket each to bring him down safely.

I don't get out much to movies for entertainment, but I do catch the news on CBC Radio and TV – if you can describe hearing about police officers charged with assault, or the ozone layer's effect on global warming, as an evening's light entertainment. At least going to bed doesn't cost me anything or bring up worries about future resources in a crowded world; not since my husband's vasectomy, anyway.

Our children are pretty entertaining. They take up much of my time, but give me back as much as they take in ideas, characterization and understanding of parts of society which I never explored before becoming a parent. The cliché is to "write what you know;" as a result, many of my characters are parents, whether in a near-future story or a fantasy world. However, clichés don't deal with the experiences of daily life which do not lend themselves to narrative flow and plot advancement. One day I'll integrate vaccination and narrow store aisles with an idealized twin stroller, and produce a Science Fiction story with broad appeal... if I can figure out whether curbs and heavy doors will still need to be navigated by strollers in the cities of the future.

I've moved away from cities to this farm, but Edmonton's lights stain the night sky even fifty miles away. I've been writing about realistic people in imaginative situations, but the faces and fashions of even contemporary Vancouver are leaving me behind. Write Science Fiction I couldn't make up a story more fantastic than tonight's news. But does the news tell us what an invention means, or how people feel? I'm trying.

Making a Joyful Noise

Ours is a marriage of mixed faiths. Many are, these days, and understanding your spouse's religion may be one heck of a lot easier than deciding about your children's religious education. Of course, it is easier if you have complementary faiths, such as when my friend married the son of an Anglican Archdeacon. "No problem about the service," she told the tight-lipped in-laws. "I'm Unitarian. We use Anglican services frequently, because they're traditional and beautiful." Instant marital bliss and family blending.

But I had to marry a pagan. Oh, Bernie gets along extremely well with my non-denominational Christianity. He generally doesn't attend church, though. So, what about our children, and their religious training? Mostly we try to integrate daily experiences and the Bible into the children's lives. There is always a need for a religious community, though.

Before we moved from the working harbour area of Victoria to rural Alberta, I tried attending services at the big church in our downtown neighbourhood. The children and I were welcome but were also mobbed by the small congregation of senior citizens. We didn't feel relaxed, or a sense of community. In addition, there were no other children present.

That improved when we moved to the farm north of Edmonton, and Bernie's parents began taking the kids and I to services in a little old country church. The twins have begun looking forward to Sunday School, and the other day asked if we were going again. Their Oma asked them what they liked best about church.

"Is it the singing?" she asked. "Or the story the minister tells the children? Or maybe you like the Sunday School picture books best?"

The children consulted briefly before reporting that what they liked best of all was sitting with their Oma in the car and eating her Clorets gum. I guess a comfortable feeling is what you make it, wherever it comes from. And if that's where they feel loving kindness and a sense of community, it's a start.

After all, the kids also like working with their father to make seasonal bonfires. Fires to mark the equinox or solstice have come down into common practice via the Yule log or Hallowe'en / Guy Fawkes bonfires. Anyone can enjoy sitting in a circle around a fire, with a hot cup in one hand and a marshmallow in the other. Actually, I don't think the marshmallows are required, but the new pagans seem to be a pretty accommodating sort. Bernie certainly is.

We ended up just before Hallowe'en this year with fourteen people of varying ages around the bonfire in our field. Together we drank over a gallon of hot chocolate, and more froze in the pot that chilly evening. While thawing out marshmallows over the coals, we took an informal poll and counted a minimum of six faiths: Catholic, Protestant, Hindu, Sikh, non-denominational Christian, and Pagan. We called it an ecumenical meeting and eventually went indoors to thaw our feet and bob for apples.

In general, apple-bobbing and eating Clorets gum are still our kids' favourite things to do, in church or out of it. But we're feeling more of a sense of community in the wide world these days, and the children are learning respect for all Creation. I may never attend my daughter's confirmation service, or watch my son learn to wind a turban. But there are still precious moments to remember. One is the twins' baptism and blessing; another is a moment among last year's asparagus.

I was cutting asparagus spears when the kids asked how asparagus knows how to come out of the ground. I told them vegetables were made that way, that asparagus grows toward the light and the warmth, and if we take care of the plants they will make food for us for a long time. When I turned round the kids were hunkered down, kissing asparagus sprouts, saying, "Thank you, Brother Asparagus. Thank you, God, for Sister Asparagus."

So religious experiences are what you make of them, wherever you find them. Between church and the Bible, and life in the wide world, there's a lot of religious education for our kids – plus two godmothers who ensure a little continuity with those who do not kiss asparagus.

As for our marriage of mixed faiths, Bernie says that even Christians can go out in the fields and do what pagans do to ensure the fields grow good crops; we just have to wait for Spring and warmer weather.

Keeping a Children's Garden,
or
Ye Joys of Gardening Pleasantlie Open'd to Tender Wits

Gardening is a real labour of love for some people, and sharing our gardens with our kids is a real joy. Our first garden was small: one spaghetti squash under a rhododendron bush. It produced a succession of male blooms and no fruit, until one magic morning when a female flower bloomed at the end of the vine. The kids and I ran inside, got a Qtip and ran back out to pollinate the flower. We played bumble bee, buzzing happily, and three weeks later, harvested our single pallid pet squash.

Our second garden was larger, just over three acres at first and expanding later, cultivated with a tractor and a rotary-tiller. The kids couldn't help much with this market garden. Instead, I spaded up a raised bed about five by twelve for the six-year-old twins to keep as their very own garden. By themselves. (You may laugh, but I learned better.)

Gardening begins with spading the earth. I didn't get much help from the kids – spades are too big for little hands. They did, however, dart in and pick worms out of the earth as it was turned. Soon they had a bucketful of rescued worms to put back into the garden before planting.

"Where are the worms?" I asked, looking around. "In a minute, Mom," one twin answered. "Worms are fun." I couldn't tell which twin it was, there was that much dirt scattered about. I had to hose them both down with well water before we went inside, or we'd have brought half the garden indoors with us that day.

Planting seeds was something we did together. None of us wanted to miss out, and besides, I had to keep the kids from eating the seeds. Some seeds are coated or treated with candy-coloured fertilizers, or poisons to prevent mold. I read all the labels on the seed packets, and began an organic method garden, without using any chemical sprays, fertilizers or weedkillers.

Weeding is one of the perpetual chores that is awfully tempting to trick the kids into doing. Unfortunately, the twins' attention span is shorter than mine. And until they learn to tell a weed from a plant, any weeding the kids do will be under the watchful eye and cracking whip of a parent for a few minutes at a time, before the baseball games.

A garden is a space in the yard, part of real lives and, as such, subject to kids running about playing ball in the carrots, or digging for gold among the potatoes. There's only so much scolding that can be stomached by me or the kids. Soon I was wondering how to ask Bernie for assistance.

"Can you build a fence? Say, about six feet high? With a sloping roof so toys don't go over it, and clear, so sunlight shines through? Uh, too much like a glass greenhouse. Forget it."

We adjusted to footprints on the lettuce, so long as they stayed out of my poppies and amaranth.

It's hard to keep cool when the kids go through the garden like a herd of locusts, picking all the produce. In our garden, the kids could eat all the sugar snap peas they wanted, but the market garden, with its cash crops, was verboten. Oh, there were days when lunch went uneaten by groaning kids, their bellies full of raw carrots and peas. There were also the days when Bernie and I came in, hot and sweaty, to find the table set and beaming children serving us scrubbed carrots and lettuce and sugar snap pea salad.

The kids had learned pride early, in their own garden. They didn't learn everything as easily. Ben made Kool-aid with hot water, and Lila set the knives on the left and the forks on the right. But we all ate and drank with a real feeling of satisfaction.

Some of the basic concepts of gardening just don't sink in with a child's first garden. It is possible for our kids to wait patiently, watching a zucchini grow, while squatting on the radishes I wanted for a salad that night. Learning is a gradual process, like gardening itself; one day's growth at a time, just like the accumulation of a compost pile. Some days my six-year-olds learned to walk around, not over plants, and some days I learned how to teach a way to pick bush beans.

"You reach under the leaves like this, see?" I tried to explain. "Don't stand on the kohlrabi plants, Ben. The beans hang down here, and – "

"What's a kohlrabi?" Ben wanted to know, looking around.

"It's like fat broccoli stems with no flowers, and you're standing on it. The beans are hanging down here by the stems, you can see them if you look-"

"Do I like kohlrabi?" Lila asked. "It looks weird."

"You like raw broccoli. You'll like kohlrabi," I told her. "Now LOOK UNDER HERE for the BEANS." I took a deep breath. Bending over at the waist like this made me dizzy and snappish. I knelt down. "You grab the bean where it joins the stem, and pull a little."

The whole plant came up in my hands. "Uh... Don't do this. You see how easy it was? Don't pull this hard. Here, you can eat all the beans on this plant and give the rest of it to the chickens." They ran off, pulling sweet tiny beans and pencil-thick bean pods off the plant, while I tried to figure out how I could pick beans all last summer for my husband's brother and still manage to yank this plant out by the roots. Maybe I should have said, "Kids! Don't try this at home! I'm a trained professional bean picker, and I still sometimes pull the plant up by the roots!"

Each year with our children we put down more roots as a family. And next year's garden is going to be even better, I'm sure, because Bernie is going to help with the spading.

The School Bus is Coming! Panic in the Street!

Our mornings have been run under a very strict schedule since September. Oh, the alarm clock may or may not get us all out of bed precisely on time. Breakfast may start early or late, and be pancakes or peanut butter on bread. There may even be time to listen to the radio news or glance at the paper I never got around to reading yesterday.

But one thing is for sure. There's always the wild run to catch the school bus. It's not because we're always late and Lisa, the bus driver, is honking the horn at the end of our driveway. We aren't always late... anymore... now that we've gotten used to booting the kids out the door to school at 7:45 am.

No, the wild run is something the kids do for fun now. Boots and coats get jammed on, knapsacks slung over shoulders, and both kids yowl and screech as they run to the side of the gravel road and look down the hill to watch for the bus. "I got here first!" yells Lila, or some mornings she calls back to the house: "You're gonna be la-ate, the bus is coming now!"

This is not the high point of my morning. I confess that, in desperation to get the kids bundled and out the door on time, I have sent the kids to school wearing odd socks. Or my T-shirts. Or their father's toques and mitts on cold mornings. But the day my son wore one white sneaker and one black sneaker was entirely his own fault. I knew nothing about it till he came home at 4:00 pm with his shoelaces untied.

"Oh, that?" he asked, with all the nonchalance of a worldly seven-year-old. "A lot of kids liked it and are going to wear two different shoes tomorrow." Oh great! Now the other parents are going to be sure I'm a bad influence. They are already suspicious because I kept my maiden name and have long hair. Sending my kid to school in two different shoes will confirm it.

While these gloomy thoughts occupied my mind, Ben was rummaging in his knapsack. "Oh yeah, here you go, Mom. I need you to sign this permission slip for tomorrow's trip to the museum." That certainly distracted me from my worries. A permission slip to sign the night before a school trip? Usually papers to sign get handed to me when both kids are stuffing lunch bags and hunting down missing boots while the bus driver is honking the horn.

To tell the truth, life isn't always that hectic for us in the mornings. In fact, when I had signed the previous permission slip one morning, I relaxed and took time to sit down with it and a cup of tea only to hear my kids yelp, "Mom! A coyote is in the yard and it's biting our ducks!" It was, too. Right under the kitchen window.

Coyotes are shy and this one ran away as I shouted. For the next few weeks I waited with the kids at the end of the driveway, talking loudly and singing songs so the coyote wouldn't come out of the bush. Then the talking loudly part came to be part of the kids' morning routine while waiting for the bus.

Lila has it down to a science. Go out on to the porch and screech: "Run and hide, Sister Coyote." Come back indoors, put on coat and boots, grab knapsack. Go outside, swinging knapsack around head, hollering "Here I come! Go hide in the bush! Here come the humans!" Then she stands at the end of the driveway, sings Whitney Houston songs and dances until the bus comes.

She is in no danger from a coyote attack. The coyotes are hiding in their dens half a mile away, wondering what all the racket is. I, however, am in danger of a heart attack if I don't quit laughing.

Ben isn't any help as I am trying to control my laughter. He methodically stomps his way through every puddle from the house to the road. Wet puddles, muddy puddles or frozen solid. He stomps them all. He can be tracked by the deep footprints he leaves behind. All this mud, ice and rainwater make quite an impression on the bus driver. Lisa cleans her bus every day, because of puddle-stompers like my son.

Oh yes, "puddle-stompers", plural. Lisa drives fifty-some kids to and from school every day. She picks them up each at their own driveways, drives them over gravel roads and a secondary highway to two schools, then picks them up from the schools and drops them off at their own driveways again. And you know what? Mostly they're pretty darn good kids for her. I'm impressed. She's better at driving more than fifty kids than I'd ever be. I have trouble navigating the crowded school parking lot on those mornings when my two kids miss the bus.

So we make the effort to catch the bus each morning, and not keep Lisa waiting. It's easier than driving the kids to school myself, and Lisa deserves not to have to wait, honking her horn at the end of the driveway. Hey, when I went along on that bus trip to the museum, I learned that driving a crowd of kids with fragrant peanut butter sandwiches down highways full of gravel trucks and hot sports cars is a hero's work. Bus drivers deserve all the respect they can get!

Were You Talking to Me?

There aren't many chances to take a break when the kids are around. Sometimes I nod off for a few minutes, sitting up in a kitchen chair while dinner is cooking. But there are some things my kids say, just as I'm nodding off for a nap, which do not inspire any further relaxation.

"DID IT WORK? DID IT work? It DID work. ...Well, maybe she's going deaf."

"I BET IT'D LOOK REAL cool if YOU were the one almost eaten by the dinosaur."

"IT WASN'T A FROG ON my head, it was a cricket. I was trying to get him to sing to me."

"MY PET WORM. HIS FAVOURITE crawling space is my necklace."

"GET OFF MY HEAD. I ASKED you to get OFF my head. It's MY head, get OFF it!"

"OOPS. WELL, IT'S NOT TOO bad. I can wipe up the part that spilled." (By the way, he didn't.)

"OOPS." (ANYTIME I HEAR this, I'm awake. Instantly!)

The Hammock

The long days of summer just laze by, the voices of children playing happily barely heard above the drone of honeybees... It sounds more like a dream than most of the summers I've had the last few years.

Summer means working in our market garden, hoeing, weeding or picking peas, beans and carrots for the farmers' markets. It means working in any weather, even when the kids are bored and whiny or playing "Peregrine Falcon" with the chickens. (This is the twins' latest game: putting a young chicken on either shoulder and one on the handlebars of a bike, then zooming around the yard at top speed. I have no idea what the chickens think of this afterward, as they stagger and flutter slowly back to the chicken house.)

Finding something for the kids to do, after they helped a little in the garden, was no longer a problem once Bernie hung a large hammock between two trees. Success! The kids clambered in, rocking the afternoon away. They invented new games, such as using clothespins to zip themselves up like bananas inside the hammock, hanging underneath like a gibbon, and trying to swing hard enough to turn upside down or completely around.

It was the game, "Dump my brother out because it's my turn" which convinced us to hang a second hammock among the trees. That, and the pleasure of taking a turn ourselves.

If you have never tried a hammock, I recommend it. The ones with wooden stretchers at both ends, which you lie on from end to end, are nice enough, though tippy. But the South American hammocks are much better. Luxuriously large, each of our hammocks is large enough for two or three kids to lie across the width of the bright Venezuelan fabric. And these hammocks are so stable and comfortable, they became our favourite place to rest after a hard day's work in the garden.

The kids had their chance to rock in the hammocks while we were busy with the hoes and rotary tiller. When it was time for a break from gardening, the kids got an object lesson in sharing.

Sometimes "sharing" means two kids share one hammock while Daddy takes his woodworking magazine into the other. Sometimes "sharing" means it's Mommy and Daddy's turn to have a hammock each for a while – and the kids' turn to go play "Peregrine Falcon" with the chickens again.

We spent the best hours of summer with a glass of lemonade, reading *House* or the journals of Lucy Maud Montgomery, rocking in arboreal bliss.

One day Lisa, the kids' bus driver, dropped by with her kids. The little, old house was a mess, of course, the yard was scattered with toys and vegetable containers drying in the sun, and even the garden ran wild with weeds. But as she got out of her pick-up truck, I steered her to a hammock and sent Ben to get lemonade. Lisa lay back, rocking in dappled green light under the treehouse where her daughters were playing with Lila.

"What a nice place you have here," she said. She was right.

My Weekend Started Tuesday Afternoon

It's been an unsettling week. We had a house guest, a trip to the Emergency Ward, and the muffler fell off the car. After all that, it was definitely time for the weekend, and it was only Tuesday.

On Monday, our house guest, Marc, arrived by bus, so we drove into Edmonton to get him, then back to the farm, giving our friend a scenic tour of the very flat Highway 28. Then the kids played with "Unca Marc" and watched TV while I chopped vegetables to put in the wok. Having a guest had made it worthwhile to run about, madly cleaning house, I had decided, and it would also made cooking dinner a lot more enjoyable.

Wrong! I heard a startled cry, and Ben turned to me with tears in his eyes. "Mom, I'm real sorry to have to tell you this," he began, "but I was playing with the plastic fish eggs from Daddy's tackle box, and I put one in my ear and I can't get it out."

I couldn't even yell at him, just stood there with my jaw hanging open, before laying him down in a sunbeam so I could look into his ear. Sure enough, there it was: a pinkish rubbery ball. And it wouldn't come out. Dinner went off the heat and we called the doctor.

That's how we ended up taking Marc on a scenic tour of Highway 2, also very flat, on our way to Emergency. Our family doctor had said not to panic, but since Ben had a cold (of course he had a cold!) the ball should be removed right away. The doctor and nurses on duty thought so, too, and used an impressive array of tools and syringes trying to get the slippery little ball out. A few tears later, Ben made earnest promises never, ever, to stick anything in his ears or nose again, and we left for home with a prescription for antibiotic ear-drops.

Where was Marc during all this? Reading old magazines in the waiting room with Lila, of course, and making wisecracks to my son, like: "Can I have the ear for my collection?" and, "Next time you want attention, yell into your Mother's ear instead of sticking something into yours."

We got back to dinner two hours late after another scenic drive along Secondary Highway 645, which is not so flat, since it crosses a river. So far we had spent over three hours of Marc's planned 23 hour visit in the car. He took it in good humour, talking a mile a minute while I drove, grimly clutching the wheel. Over dinner I told the kids that they were never to do that again, but I was happy to have been told right away.

Ben rubbed his sore ear. "It worked out pretty well, Mom," he said. "I didn't have to wait long, and they got the ball right out, even though it broke all in pieces."

"Oooh, yeah. That's why I took another one along," I nodded. "They're kind of slippery, and I wanted the doctor to see what it looked like, and how big – "

"—is Ben's brain," Marc finished the sentence.

Next morning after the scramble to get the kids and their lunches onto the school bus, I drove Marc to meet his ride in the nearby town. After dropping him off, I hit a rough spot in the road. Sure enough, the muffler came loose. I stopped at a friend's house, called a mechanic, and got right back on the road... after a quick cup of tea and a twenty-minute chat about the dubious merits of voting for any of the candidates in the coming provincial election. Back on the road, I looked in the rear-view mirror and saw flashing red and blue lights. Why not?

When I pulled over, the Mountie walked up beside my open window. "Did you know your muffler is making a lot of noise?" he asked, then answered his own question. "Of course...you...must...know that." He must have seen my face as I sat, praying silently that I wouldn't get a ticket or fine. I'd spent all my money for the month on gasoline during all the scenic touring. "Are you going to get it fixed?" he asked gently. "You have to be careful about exhaust getting inside the car, you know."

"I'm on my way to the mechanic now," I said, relieved that the Mountie's ticket book was staying in his coat pocket. "My window and vent are open, and I'll watch out for exhaust smells."

The Mountie gave me a friendly smile and waved me on my way to the mechanic, whose bill was both smaller than I expected, and large enough to take all the cash I had on hand. (Do mechanics have X-ray vision or something?)

Next I had to drive to another town (along Secondary Highway 651, very boggy gravel and no scenery) to go to the bank and the drug store for my son's prescription eardrops, which I had almost forgotten. I will never forget them again. Twenty-two dollars for eight mililitres of ear drops. At that price, he might as well be dabbing the drops behind his ears. But even perfume doesn't cost that much!

I went home and got into a nice, hot bath. My weekend started Tuesday afternoon, whatever the calendar says. And if anyone comes looking for me before Sunday, I'm liable to be in the bathtub...still.

Things I'm Grateful For This Thanksgiving

Those Sunday mornings I couldn't crawl out of bed and my kids made toast and tea and brought it to me on a tray.

WHEN MY SPOUSE WENT to take a course for ten months I had to do all the driving in town and on the farm – and my highway speed went up from 80 km/h to the speed limit.

WHEN I CALLED MY MOTHER long distance this spring to apologize for every bit of grief I ever put her through when I was a kid, she lied and said, "You were a wonderful child. You never gave us a moment's grief."

WHEN MY SON CUT APART the box holding his prized comic book collection and lined it with old towels to make a bed for his sister's new kitten.

MOVING BACK TO VICTORIA! Visiting the farm in summer!

WHEN MY BROTHER AND sister-in-law's dogs were expecting puppies, I could take the dogs for walks when they were at work, finally returning some kind of favour for all they do for us.

IF IT WEREN'T FOR LILA begging for a kitten, I'd never have learned how much warmer it is typing with a cat on my lap.

How to Have Fun With a Cat

Take the toddlers to a friend's house, where they play with a cat. "Cats are nice, Mama. I yove cats." Rescue the cat from under a cushion and let it hide under the chesterfield. Console the kids by letting them refill the cat's bowls with fresh water and crunchies. Wipe up the spills.

Visit the twins' godparents who have many cats and must have hidden in their basement a litterbox the size of a waterbed. "Can I have a kitty, Mommy? Arwen has five. I only want one of my very own," begs my daughter.

"Did you see their big grey cat's eyes?" asks my son. "And he growls! He's like the comic book Uncle Dan gave me, with Destructo and the mutants."

Drink tea with a friend's cat curled on my lap. This cat's best friend is a bunny rabbit who leaves pellets under the chairs and has intimate relations with balloons. Reflect that cats aren't that bad by comparison, especially when the balloon pops.

Promise my daughter a cat. Apologize to my husband. Visit a few kittens, eventually find one that's healthy, good natured, pretty, and only ten bucks. The kids are delighted and hug her and pet her and put the harness ($) on her and feed her (more $) and show her all over the house. Shadow sleeps alone the first few nights, then decides Lila's room and bed are nicer.

Why did I get a black-and-white kitten when most of my clothes are either black or white?

Everything is accented with cat hairs now – white on the black clothes, black on the white.

Watch kids play with kitten, feed it, hug it while watching TV, make toys for it, help clean its litterbox and fight over who takes it to bed. Having a cat is good for the kids and definitely better than giving them a younger sibling so they can learn to share and care for another living being. Besides, cats have claws and don't put up with much nonsense.

The kitten is missing one night at bedtime.

Look everywhere and give up. Put kids to bed, take flashlights and look around the neighbourhood.

Bernie wakes up early to look before the kids get up. No cat anywhere until our son opens his dresser drawers, where he finds a flat, dizzy kitten in among his underwear.

Instead of watching mindless TV shows, watch the kitten watching TV. Her scrabbles and wiggles are more entertaining. When this palls, put the cat in front of the aquarium. Fish TV has a lot more appeal for Shadow, and sometimes the goldfish come over to the glass and look at her. Are they staring at this black-and-white monster or chanting, "Naah, naah naah naa-naa?" Our laughter disturbs the kitten, and she glares at us, haughty.

My son puts a marble, a golf ball and the cat into an empty laundry basket inventing a toy that keeps the cat busy for hours, day after day. I learn to take the noisy marble out at night.

Answer the door, find wallet and pay courier for a package, keeping door shut so cat will stay indoors.

Go looking for cat afterward. Cat has stolen a ball of yarn and tangled it around and around a table and chairs. Cat is attempting to carry off yarn like a small dead animal, but whichever way she goes, there is no escape.

Give the kitten a bundle of catnip. She scrabbles around the kitchen, attacking the ankles of anyone cooking or washing dishes. Bounding into the living room, she sharpens her claws on the furniture and leaps back into the dining room, sliding off the chairs. Take back the catnip and advise her, "Just say No."

If an old sock is left anywhere, the cat stalks and pounces on it. She carries it off like a lioness with an antelope in her jaws. If we are unimpressed by her hunting prowess, she pounces on our ankles again. A two-year-old comes to visit and the kitten's eyes widen as she ponders human prey she might actually be able to bring down in a hunt. She soon learns that toddlers are as ruthless as cats and retreats to the back of a chair, where she looks down on the lot of us, laughing on the floor with the kid. Who cares if it's evolution in action? It's fun.

Observations and Comments

Ben, looking at his grass-stained knees and hands sticky with pine sap, announced with satisfaction: "If you haven't had to wash your hands two or three times by dinner, you haven't done anything that day."

BEN CURLED UP ON THE couch under a knitted blanket, in front of the television. "Next winter I want to hibernate."

"WOW, THE KITTY PURRS real loud now!" Spoken under a quilt with his head up against the kitten's rib cage.

"BE CAREFUL WITH THE kitty, Mom, she's just a baby." This from Lila, who just took the cat outdoors on a chill November morning without putting on her own shoes and coat first.

"I LIKE TO DO ABSTRACT painting," Lila explained. "I keep my eyes closed until it's almost done, then I open them and see what it is I'm painting, and then I finish it."

RUBBING HER EYES ONE morning, Lila commented: "I had nightmares, but it wasn't about the ghost story I was reading. I just wanted to keep my light on all night anyway."

WHEN HE ARRIVED HOME from school on Valentine's Day, Ben announced: "I've just had two cupcakes, three brownies, four helpings of potato chips, four glasses of pop and one of juice, and enough jellybeans and candy hearts to make a camel barf. So I'm not hungry for a snack."

LILA HAD A BAD COLD and stayed home from school. Stumbling from bed to the bathroom, she asked Bernie in a froggy hoarse voice: "Am I gonna live?"

"I'm afraid so," Bernie said seriously.

"Is my daddy teasing me again?" she croaked.

"I'm afraid so," he said again, as seriously as before.

"Daddy, I think you never grew up," she told him.

"Not all the way, honey," he agreed and hugged her. "Not for the fun bits, anyway."

BEN EMPTIED HIS POCKETS of two bottle caps, a padlock, a brass key (which didn't open the padlock, alas), a bent wire lock pick (which did, aargh – my son the lock picker), a little toy monster and a rat skull, all of which he'd found on his way home from school. "I think that eighty-five percent of the neat things you find in your life," he said, "you find before you're eight years old."

Bernie Gets The Last Word, or
YES I SHAVED MY KID'S HEAD
and Other Tales of Parenting in the '90's

IT'S A BIT NERVE-WRACKING when your wife decides to write non-fiction. I mean, Paula has been writing fiction for years, and I've never had a problem. All I did was pick the best, most admirable character in the story and say, "Hey, she modeled that character after me!" But now, with non-fiction, my name is even showing up. This gets a bit scary.

Don't get me wrong. It's not that I think my life or myself might be the least bit strange or unusual. It's just that strange or unusual things tend to happen to me. And Paula writes about them. Again, that's not necessarily bad. It's just that we don't always agree on the how or why of my getting involved. ...

Take, just as an example, my son's haircut. Now I grew up during the sixties when hair was a basis for inter-generational warfare. My Dad and I fought our share of wars over hair. This is not an unusual story.

Even when I was seventeen, he won and I ended up with a brushcut. Which, many think, explains the length of my hair now (pony-tailed) but doesn't explain the short hair I wore during the mid-eighties. The long and the short of it all, however, is that I'm now very forgiving about people choosing to express their individuality by futzing around with their hair.

When he was three, Ben saw his first mohawk-style cut at a peace rally. This was not just a "boring" old mohawk. This was hair that demanded attention!

Twelve inch (that's 300mm for those who have managed the change), tri-coloured spikes grew stiff and proud out of a shaved head. Six earrings in the right ear and a jacket of gloriously-studded black leather. No pretty popster this, this was a punk vision from Thatcher's Britain, with the Pistol's "Never Mind the Bollocks" tattooed on his forebrain with glow-in-the-dark ink. And a sign that said, "Because the Children deserve to Live Too." He was standing next to his Mom.

My three-year-old was transfixed. His eyes followed the spikes the full three miles to the Legislature front lawn. Riding on my shoulders helped – there *were* a lot of people there. But Ben saw nothing else.

When the kids were about two, and were listening to all the various kid music that they listened too, I taught them Monty Python's, "The Lumberjack Song" about the joys of nonconformity and a cross-dressing lumberjack. Why? Two reasons, really. The first was that one more round of "Itsy Bitsy Spider" and I was going to end up in a bell tower with a baseball bat, and they'd eventually blame marine training. The other was that I figured that if I introduced the kids to the basic surreal nature of the modern world nice and early, they'd have less problems dealing with it later on. (Besides, I think the song is a hoot, and it's fun to sing in line-ups surrounded by unsuspecting older people).

Seems to have worked, too. The kids seem untroubled by the fact that the world is a very weird place. Although they seem to be as bothered as their parents by the *ways* in which it doesn't make sense. Like how we all talk about how nice we're supposed to be to each other, but have you experienced the playground recently? So odd haircuts should be no big deal to take in stride. And, sure enough, when I asked Ben about the hairdo, I found that he hadn't been taken aback at all. Far from it, he LOVED it.

And please Dad, how soon could he have the same 'do?

Well, Ollie. This is another fine mess you've gotten us into. I mean, I kinda liked the look myself. Tough, dangerous, committed. I impress no one as tough, I've never been thought of as dangerous, though a few people have thought I should be committed... But never mind that. What do I answer? "Well son, not at the moment. You don't really have enough hair, do you?" Thankfully, he agreed. I figured maybe he'd forget it until he was, oh, 37 or so. Then he could do what he wanted and I wouldn't have to explain it to the grandparents.

And there it was again. I would have to explain it to my folks. And that old fight could just start up again. No thanks. Let him want it, and then slowly forget it, and I'm off the hook. But he didn't forget it. Well, not for longer than a couple of months at a time. And then those damned turtles showed up.

Remember - oh yes you do - the invasion of the Teenage Mutant Ninja Turtles(tm)? Yes, I lived through them, too. But it was one of the bad guys that caught Ben's attention. This bad guy (no, thankfully I don't remember its name) did have one distinguishing feature. Yes. A mohawk. Three years those mutant ninnys hung around. Three years Ben played with that mohawked maniac. And then for the first time, the focused nature of his desire shifted.

"Dad."

"Yeah?"

"Can I shave my head bald?" Now why!

Thankfully it wasn't only my kid. We visited a friend, and his son *was* bald. Seems he'd decided that asking took too long, so he used the scissors to get himself started. Ben didn't copy him, thank goodness. But in exchange he got the closest buzzcut I'd seen since, well, since I was eleven. His grandfather loved it. Of course.

But this was only a passing fancy, it seems. Ben still wanted the mohawk. Then a few months back I saw all the kids in his class, plus the grade up, and matching grades from other schools. I relaxed. Out of a hundred different kids, there hadda be seventy-three different hair styles. And suddenly I knew. It would be okay. No one would give him any grief in the playground. Grandparents could be handled.

There really was no point in denying him this.

Even so, I couldn't yet get to the full mohawk. Everything in life moves in stages. I pulled out the razor and shaving cream and shaved the sides of his head. There was nothing but a skinny line of hair in back, and an odd-shaped mop on top. I did handle the grandparents. And I felt a lot better, too. No more evasions – incompetence in haircutting isn't an evasion, it's the truth.

So you see, when Paula started writing non-fiction, I started getting nervous. Because every time something odd happens to me, it might just end up in print. And it just might look like I meant it to happen that way....

Don't miss out!

Visit the website below and you can sign up to receive emails whenever Paula Johanson publishes a new book. There's no charge and no obligation.

https://books2read.com/r/B-A-ZKUK-ZTTBC

BOOKS 2 READ

Connecting independent readers to independent writers.

Did you love *No Parent Is An Island*? Then you should read *Green Paddler*[1] by Paula Johanson!

This book on paddlesports details using kayaks and other small boats with an eye to environmental sensibility and affordable recreation. In **Green Paddler**, author Paula Johanson reprises her short articles from *Kayak Yak* website and brings new insights & humour to the time she spends on the water.

"*Superb! What a fantastic read for a Monday morning.*" -Pearly on *AdvancedElements* kayaking forum

As a teenager, Paula learned kayaking and canoeing. After a sudden hearing loss took her sense of balance, she returned to paddling for fitness and vestibular improvement. Finding a calming oasis of nature in cities is a bonus! Whether she's at home on a west coast island or travelling in Canada to promote her writing, her kayaks make it possible for this stocky little woman to haul her own gear so she can paddle in harbours, lakes, and rivers. Though she doesn't own a car or a couch, her "Affordable Fleet" of kayaks includes folding

---

1. https://books2read.com/u/bPyaLl
2. https://books2read.com/u/bPyaLl

inflatable kayaks from AdvancedElements, as well as wheels for a Necky Eliza sea kayak and an old Pamlico to loan to beginners. "With the finely-honed body of a freelance writer, I turn heads as I bring my inflatable kayaks on buses, trains, and airplanes, or wheel my sea kayak along a road," she says. "...but it's the kayaks that get all the attention."

Doublejoy Books is thrilled to release this practical discussion of using small boats. The enjoyment of kayaking shows on every page as paddler Paula Johanson talks about how it feels to get out on the water, even when one is not a hard-body Olympian. **Green Paddler** is the author's forty-fourth nonfiction book, and her confidence is clear whether she welcomes the reader to paddlesports or environmental concerns.

"Paula's experience as a professional writer shows when writing about her prime leisure time activity, kayaking. I find myself smiling at Paula's clever descriptions of the places that she's paddled and her humorous observations about the people around her. Paula's words paint a clear picture of the places she's paddling so I can imagine being there alongside her." - Justine Curgenven, award-winning adventure filmmaker and expedition kayaker

"Great posts! It makes me want to get out on the water." -Lakejumper on *AdvancedElements* kayaking forum

Read more at books2read.com/paulaj.

Also by Paula Johanson

Alt-Academic
Woolgathering: Awareness of the Foreign in Published Works About Cowichan Woolworking

Sanitizer

Prime Ministers of Canada
Pierre Elliott Trudeau: Child of Nature

Charles Tupper: Warhorse

Slice of Life
No Parent Is An Island

Working Parent

Under The Plow

Young Science
Bat Poop Sparkles

Otters Hold Hands

Standalone

Small Rain and Other Nightmares
Island Views
Plum Tree
Tower in the Crooked Wood
King Kwong: Larry Kwong, the China Clipper Who Broke the NHL Colour Barrier
Science Critters
Green Paddler

Watch for more at books2read.com/paulaj.

About the Author

Paula Johanson is a Canadian writer. A graduate of the University of Victoria with an MA in Canadian literature, she has worked as a security guard, a short order cook, a teacher, newspaper writer, and more. As well as editing books and teaching materials, she has run an organic-method small farm with her spouse, raised gifted twins, and cleaned university dormitories. In addition to novels and stories, she is the author of forty-two books written for educational publishers, among them *The Paleolithic Revolution* and *Women Writers* from the series *Defying Convention: Women Who Changed The World*. Johanson is an active member of SF Canada, the national association of science fiction and fantasy authors.

Read more at books2read.com/paulaj.

About the Publisher

Doublejoy Books is the publisher of a variety of eclectic books of Canadian literature.
   http://doublejoybooks.com
   http://books2read.com/paulaj

www.ingramcontent.com/pod-product-compliance
Lightning Source LLC
Chambersburg PA
CBHW031647040426
42453CB00006B/238